The Audience

Peter Morgan is an international award-winning writer
for stage, screen and film. As well as receiving Oscar and
BAFTA nominations for his screenplay for Stephen Frears'
The Queen, starring Helen Mirren, Morgan won a host
of international awards including Golden Globe, British
Independent Film and *Evening Standard* British Film
Awards. His last play, the award-winning *Frost/Nixon*,
received critical acclaim on both sides of the Atlantic
before being adapted into an Academy Award-nominated
film of the same name. The film garnered five Oscar
nominations, including Best Screenplay. His many other
film credits include the award-winning *The Last King of
Scotland*, *The Damned United*, and the upcoming *Rush*,
directed by Ron Howard, as well as his current project
for Warner Bros about the life of Hugh Hefner, entitled
Playboy. His extensive television credits include the
critically acclaimed *The Deal* – the first part of Morgan's
'Tony Blair Trilogy' (BAFTA Award for Best Drama) –
The Special Relationship and *Longford*.

PETER MORGAN

The Audience

faber and faber

First published in 2013
by Faber and Faber Limited
74–77 Great Russell Street, London WC1B 3DA

Typeset by Country Setting, Kingsdown, Kent CT14 8ES
Printed in England by CPI Group (UK) Ltd, Croydon CR0 4YY

A CIP record for this book
is available from the British Library

978–0–571–30406–6

4 6 8 10 9 7 5 3

Introduction

When I started writing the screenplay for *The Queen*, about the aftermath of the death of Princess Diana, both Stephen Frears, the director, and Andy Harries, the producer, begged me not to put Tony Blair in it. They felt the presence of a politician, particularly one as divisive as Blair had become by 2004, would diminish it – make it feel more temporal, more journalistic, more TV. And so less filmic.

I consoled myself that there would still be plenty to work with: the death of a Princess, a Queen's young deputy private secretary out of his depth, a Royal Family tucked away on the Balmoral estate, and people out on the streets of London baying for blue blood. But after three months, I had written just 35 pages and wanted to shoot myself. It was awful. I rang Frears and Harries and told them the script was a big fat royalist snooze. Would never work. Everyone gracefully accepted defeat, and Frears went on to direct another movie.

Privately, however, I was deflated. I felt I hadn't given an interesting subject a fair shot. I retreated to the mountains of Austria and, without telling anyone, wrote my own version. With Blair. I didn't care if it felt smaller. I didn't care if it was journalistic, nor if it ended up on TV or radio. I wrote a draft in under three weeks. It was one of those experiences that comes all too rarely, where you hear the voices and write with total certainty. You're not really writing – you're channelling.

Looking back, I realise the reason I was suddenly so unblocked was because I had stumbled on something significant: the relationship between our most senior elected public servant and our head of state. The first minister and the crown. Two human beings, in flesh and blood, but also the representatives of their offices. At some level, just by having them sitting opposite one another, even in silence, one was dealing with the British constitution, the bone structure of our establishment in its most elemental form.

Happily, Frears liked the script and committed to filming it. As I watched Helen Mirren and Michael Sheen at work, I started thinking more about the sovereign and the PM – and the weekly 'audience' at the heart of their relationship, and what a unique opportunity it presented a dramatist. Because the meeting is so shrouded in confidentiality, imagining what was discussed felt more valid, somehow, than proving it. I resolved, as far back as 2006, to write something.

In reality, depending on the chemistry between them, the audience can either be no more than an informal briefing – a courtesy, where the PM brings the sovereign up to speed with what happened in the past week and what is expected in the following one – or it can be a great deal more. Some of the pairings have been reluctant; some eagerly looked forward to. Some of the sessions last barely twenty minutes with no refreshment; others stretch out to an hour or two – with drinks. Some PMs are grateful for the breaks provided by foreign travel; others are sure to have their audience by phone even when abroad.

So when did they start? I wrote to Professor Vernon Bogdanor, the closest thing we have to a formal constitutional expert in this country where no formal constitution exists. 'I am not wholly clear when they began,' he said. 'I do not think they existed before the war. But during the war, the practice arose of the King and Churchill meeting for regular lunches. That was a consequence of the particularly good relationship they had built up – after a shaky start. The regular meetings have now become so much of a convention they could be regarded as part of the constitution – in a typically British unplanned way. Were either the PM or the sovereign to discontinue them, this would, I think, be regarded as a breach.'

So there it is: the private audience has come in through the back door. And yet the meeting is not minuted or recorded. No one else is present. This is vital – so that PMs can feel free to say what they like, and even make disobliging remarks about colleagues. As a weekly event, it takes up a significant amount of the PM's working life. Allowing for summer breaks, an average four-year term would contain at least seventy meetings. Seventy hours! I dare say there are happy friendships, even marriages, where partners don't sit opposite one another and talk openly, in a spirit of trust and mutual confidence, for an hour a week. Indeed, the very nature of the meeting (one-on-one, confidential, one-sided) reflects another relationship: therapy. And James Callaghan did say it was like talking to one's psychiatrist.

In which case, should we not be entitled to know more about it? How has the meeting worked over the years? What form does it take? Which PMs liked to talk? Who liked to listen? Who was HM's favourite? With whom was there chemistry, laughter, silence? What did they discuss? How many secrets were shared? What advice was given? What influence did it have? The Queen is known to have struggled to stay awake with Heath and Macmillan (both famous bores), actively disliked Blair and Thatcher (though the Palace dutifully denies this), and had a soft spot for losers (two of her favourites, Major and Wilson, regularly come bottom in rankings for most effective PMs of the twentieth century).

One popular misconception might be that it's a polite chat, over scones or sherry, with the PM checking his or her watch, wanting to get on with more important business. But as Margaret Thatcher said: 'Anyone who imagines that they are a mere formality, or confined to social niceties, is quite wrong; they are quietly businesslike, and Her Majesty brings to bear a formidable grasp of current issues and breadth of experience.'

The Queen reads each one of her red ministerial boxes every day, is privy to the minutes from every cabinet meeting, has a generous staff to keep her informed, and is scrupulously prepared for every meeting. In civil service circles, she is known as 'Reader Number 1'. A meeting with Her Majesty, therefore, is like a meeting with a well-briefed civil servant. If transcripts of the audience were to exist, I'm confident she would emerge with some credit.

It struck me that by being denied the minutes of these conversations, we were being denied a significant part of British history: an insight into the workings of government and state, and the way power – real and symbolic – functions in our name. In the nineteenth century, the essayist Walter Bagehot argued that the Queen has three constitutional rights: the right to be consulted, the right to advise, and the right to warn. No more. But bear in mind she spends an hour every week sitting one-on-one with the most important politician in Britain. How much has she known over the years that has been denied us? How much has she known that we haven't?

The longer she remains on the throne, the greater her standing on the world stage and the greater the respect for her – and, therefore, the greater her potential surreptitious influence. Imagine you're Ed Miliband: you've narrowly won the election, and you go to the Queen to ask her permission to form a government. The idea that the most instantly recognisable woman in the world – who has sat opposite Churchill, Eden, Macmillan, Douglas-Home, Wilson, Heath, Callaghan, Thatcher, Major, Blair, Brown, Cameron, presided over a Commonwealth and had a ringside seat at the great political events of the second half of the twentieth century – would not have influence on you is laughable, simply by virtue of your anxiety at least to leave an impression. You don't want to be the one she forgets.

That gives her influence, if not power. And any influence over our PM needs to be examined closely. So I set about writing a series of what must strictly be called 'imagined' audiences (although no shortage of anecdotal information has leaked out over the years) between the Queen and her various PMs – and was immediately presented with a challenge. How could one tell the story without it feeling linear and inevitable? How could one avoid the almost audible ticking off in theatregoers' heads as PMs came on and off the stage? Nothing is enjoyable if there is no sense of surprise – and everyone knows who they all were, even if they can't quite remember all their names.

So I decided to tell it in a non-linear way, leaving out some PMs. Who to drop and why? I wrestled long and hard with this and, as we head into rehearsals, I have made my decisions. But by curtain-up, it might be totally different. Who knows?

Peter Morgan

This article first appeared in *The Guardian* on 14 January 2013, and is reprinted by kind permission.

The Audience was first produced at the Gielgud Theatre, London, on 15 February 2013, presented by Matthew Byam Shaw, Robert Fox and Andy Harries. The cast was as follows:

Queen Elizabeth II Helen Mirren
Sir Anthony Eden Michael Elwyn
Margaret Thatcher Haydn Gwynne
Harold Wilson Richard McCabe
Gordon Brown Nathaniel Parker
John Major Paul Ritter
David Cameron Rufus Wright
Winston Churchill Edward Fox
James Callaghan/Private Secretary David Peart
Equerry Geoffrey Beevers
Young Elizabeth Bebe Cave, Maya Gerber, Nell Williams
Bobo MacDonald/Private Secretary Charlotte Moore
Junior Equerries/Footmen Harry Feltham, Matt Plumb
Queen's Dressers Spencer Kitchen, Elaine Solomon
Cecil Beaton/Detective Jonathan Coote
Detective/Policeman Ian Houghton

Director Stephen Daldry
Designer Bob Crowley
Lighting Designer Rick Fisher
Sound Designer Paul Arditti
Video Designer Ian William Galloway
Composer Paul Englishby
Hair and Wigs Designer Ivana Primorac

Characters

Queen Elizabeth II
Young Elizabeth
Winston Churchill
Anthony Eden
Harold Wilson
James Callaghan
Margaret Thatcher
John Major
Gordon Brown
David Cameron
Equerry
Bobo Macdonald
Dressers
Private Secretaries
Detectives

THE AUDIENCE

Act One

A darkened stage. Bare. The Queen's Equerry-in-Waiting,
a Lieutenant-Commander LVO Royal Navy, walks on.
  Black military uniform, with braided gold cord on the
right shoulder, red stripe on the side of the trousers.
  On his shoulders, small black epaulettes with a gold
crown and the sovereign's insignia as a fastener. One or
two medals. He turns to face the audience.

Equerry Every Tuesday, at approximately 6.30 p.m., the
Queen of the United Kingdom has a private audience
with her Prime Minister. It is not an obligation. It is a
courtesy extended by the Prime Minister, to bring Her
Majesty up to speed. The meeting takes place in the
Private Audience Room located on the first floor of
Buckingham Palace.

  The Equerry turns, indicating the darkened space.

A large, duck-egg blue room. High ceilings, a fireplace,
a Chippendale bureau. Four gilt-framed paintings, two by
Canaletto, two by Gainsborough. At the centre of the
room, two chairs made by François Hervé, in 1826. Their
original colour was burgundy, but Queen Mary had them
re-upholstered in more optimistic yellow Dupioni silk.
One drawback to the yellow is that it stains easily, and
the chairs have needed several refreshments. According to
household records, they were last re-upholstered in a
yellow that almost matched the original on 13th January
1995.

  The Equerry walks off.
  As he goes, we reveal the audience room, with two
yellow chairs. Freshly upholstered.

In one chair is the sixty-nine year old Queen
Elizabeth II. Opposite her is John Major, fifty-two.
Her ninth Prime Minister.

Major I only ever wanted to be ordinary.

A silence. The Queen stares.

Elizabeth And in which way do you consider you've
failed in that ambition?

Major What's going on in my political life at the moment
is just so *extra*ordinary. My government is tearing itself
apart. I withdrew the whip from eight of my backbenchers
in an attempt to restore party discipline, but it's achieved
nothing. When they're not out there on College Green
briefing against me morning and night they seem to be
engaged in a never-ending game of political hara-kiri.
And the papers are being so vile . . .

Elizabeth It's a dangerous business, reading newspapers.
Most of your predecessors claimed not to, and I can't
help thinking that's wise.

Major I know. I just can't help myself. Can't walk past
one of the things without picking it up, hoping for a lift.
And then I get crushed when they're so . . . mean. Most
of my political life it was fine because I was generously
overlooked. I was barely mentioned as Foreign Secretary,
nor as Chancellor. Did you know eighteen months before
I became Prime Minister just two per cent of the country
had even heard of me?

Elizabeth Beware the quiet man!

Major Beware the Invisible Man! When I walk into a
room, heads fail to turn.

Elizabeth (*sighs*) How lovely . . .

Major I remember how my heart sank when I was asked
to take the Foreign Office. And when Margaret told me

4

she wanted me to be the 'centrepiece' of her reshuffle . . .
I almost ran away. To be thrust like that. Into the
spotlight.

Elizabeth So why on earth did you run for Prime
Minister?

Major I did it reluctantly, I assure you. With a heavy
heart. And never expected to win. And now with all these
problems.

Elizabeth What problems, Mr Major? We're not at war.
The people aren't on the streets.

Major No, but ten-per-cent interest rates, the fallout
from Black Wednesday, an increasingly belligerent anti-
European caucus – it's hardly a happy ship, either. My
polls ratings are at a historic low.

Elizabeth There are summits and there are valleys. We've
all been there.

Major Twenty-four-per-cent approval, Ma'am?! You've
never been anywhere close.

Elizabeth I beg to differ. And you should remember
better than anyone. That day . . . in December? Three
years ago.

Major You were unwell that day.

Elizabeth It was just a cold..

Major It was flu, Ma'am.

Elizabeth Cold . . .

Major You were running a fever. The Equerry was quite
clear...

Elizabeth IT WAS A COLD!

Major Quite. And long forgotten now.

Elizabeth It will *never* be forgotten. What you did. Nor the help you gave me. You proved yourself a loyal ally to m— (*Wants to say 'me', but checks herself.*) – this family. Which is why I am keen to help you in return.

She thinks.

You could always resign?

Major Don't think I hadn't considered it. Resign at lunchtime, at Lord's by the afternoon. I'd be happy as Bunter in a bakery.

Elizabeth In order to stand again. For re-election?

Major (*heart sinks*) Oh.

Elizabeth Throw down a gauntlet. To all those nasty rebels.

Major 'Sack me or back me.'

Elizabeth Something like that.

Major 'Put up or shut up.'

Elizabeth Even better. A real show of strength.

For a moment Major's face is re-energised. Then it falls again.

Major But what if they *did* back me? We'd only be back here again in a month.

Elizabeth Mr Major, I detect you're a man who is uncomfortable in his own crisis – yet you were so good in mine. Which places you at a distinct disadvantage. Since from where I've been sitting all these years it seems crisis in your job is the natural setting. At some point *all* your predecessors have been hated, or rejected. By their own party. By the electorate.

Major What an awful job.

Elizabeth But they fight against it. Turn it around. To their own advantage.

Major Perhaps because they're more aggressive personality types. Better suited to be Prime Minister. Someone told me once inhumanity is a primary requirement of the top job.

Elizabeth For the most part I've found my Prime Ministers to be very human. (*A beat.*) All *too* human. Complicated souls. Having suffered early parental bereavement. Or illness. Or depression. Or bullying in the corridors of Eton . . .

Major Ah. Not me. Rutlish Grammar.

Elizabeth Which part of the world is that?

Major Merton Park.

From the Queen's blank look:

Near Morden?

Another blank look.

Raynes Park? (*A beat.*) A suburb of south-west London, Ma'am. Near Mitcham?

A beat.

Elizabeth Never been. Pity.

A beat, then:

At least you *had* a formal education. I wasn't that lucky.

Major You were at home? With a tutor?

Elizabeth Yes.

Major I'm curious. Was that because you were . . . female?

Elizabeth You're ahead of me, Prime Minister. I was banking on the idea that I still am.

7

Major I meant the home education?

Elizabeth You mean had we been boys would we have been sent to boarding school?

Major Yes.

Elizabeth Probably.

Major So, you and your sister were victims of gender discrimination?

Elizabeth I suppose we were. Do you think I should sue?

Major smiles.

We weren't expected to excel. Just to be decorous, be able to dance, draw and speak French at mealtimes. Not what you'd call a progressive syllabus, but quite normal for the time.

Major When I read about the home education, I didn't know whether to envy or pity you.

Elizabeth I suppose that depends on whether you have happy memories of your own time at school or not.

Major Not so happy, I'm afraid. You may know, my father performed in a circus . . .

Elizabeth (*brightening*) Yes. A trapeze artist, am I right?

Major Yes.

Elizabeth How wonderful.

Major (*bemused*) Wonderful?

Elizabeth Well, it's just so . . . exotic.

Major Your father was King of England, and Emperor of India. If I may say, *that's* exotic.

The Queen smiles.

Anyway, when he left the circus my father embarked on a career producing garden ornaments.

Elizabeth How lovely.

A beat. Her expression changes.

What exactly *are* garden ornaments?

Major Decorative statuettes, Ma'am.

Elizabeth Oh, statues. (*Understanding now.*) We have plenty of those.

Major I doubt you have gnomes.

Elizabeth We have a statue of George IV. Does that count? He was barely five foot.

Major Anyway, my father's actual surname was Ball, but when he joined the circus he decided to take the stage name 'Major'. When I was accepted by Rutlish and catapulted into the high society of Merton Park, he insisted I fuse stage and birth names and call myself –

Can hardly bring himself to say it.

Elizabeth Ball-Major?

Major Regrettably the other way round. So schooldays were marked somewhat by bullying and ridicule.

Elizabeth Oh, dear. How did you cope? You immersed yourself in studies, I expect?

Major Cricket. It was what I was good at. Afraid academic work and I didn't see eye to eye. I believe I have the dubious distinction of being the only Prime Minister to have – (*He looks up.*) Will what I'm about to tell you stay between us?

Elizabeth Prime Minister, everything you say in this room stays between us.

Major Three O-levels. A miserable failure that must have been quite devastating to my parents. Through sheer idleness and disinterest I let them down. And when I went home with those *dreadful* results, you could see the hurt on their faces . . . (*Becoming emotional.*) But there was no reproach. Ever.

Major's eyes fill with tears as he relives a private trauma. The Queen stares. Aghast.

Elizabeth Well, I have no O-levels at all. (*A beat.*) What fine hands the country is in. Now we have only a few minutes left, we really must get to the business in hand. You returned from the G7 last week and we haven't even mentioned it, and you're due in Cannes next week for a Heads of European Government meeting and I want to know all about that.

Major Well, starting with the G7, we received a very warm welcome from our Canadian hosts – since if you remember we'd taken their side over a recent fishing dispute . . .

Elizabeth Which fish?

Major I believe the turbot, Ma'am.

Elizabeth That's a flat fish, isn't it?

Major Yes, Ma'am.

Elizabeth With eyes in the middle of its head?

Major Yes.

Elizabeth Like the halibut.

Major I believe it *is* a halibut.

Elizabeth Oh.

Major It's just marketed as Greenland turbot in America to prevent any confusion with the Pacific halibut.

Elizabeth (*not seeing*) I see.

Major However in Europe we call it Greenland halibut not to confuse it with the *real* turbot.

Elizabeth It's like the Duke of Normandy also being called the Lord of Mann.

Major I dare say.

Elizabeth Or the Duke of Lancaster being called the Lord High Admiral of the Royal Navy.

Major I'll take your word for it. I'm afraid I don't know these people.

Elizabeth Actually you do. You've met them all. In fact you're sitting with them now. They're all me. And some of my other titles.

Major Oh.

Elizabeth Kotoku, the 'White Heron', Paramount Chief of Fiji. Me, too!

Major The real turbot.

Elizabeth Yes. Just with slightly more attractively positioned eyes.

As they walk off, lights change, the stage is plunged into darkness.

The Equerry walks on.

Equerry Audiences between the Queen and Prime Minister take place every Tuesday evening and this has been the case with each of Her Majesty's PMs – with the exception of her tenth.

While the Equerry speaks, an august, elderly silhouette wearing top hat and frock coat, walks across the stage.

Equerry He suggested that the audience be moved to Wednesday evenings – to allow him time to better prepare for Prime Minister's Questions. The Queen expressed 'surprise' at this break with tradition, and was comforted when Mr Blair finally left office, hoping that the audiences could be moved back to Tuesdays again. At 6.30 p.m. As they had been, right from the beginning . . .

Winston Churchill removes his hat, white-faced, bows deeply in deference (with difficulty, wheezing conspicuously, clearly experiencing discomfort), then straightens . . .

But evolution stops for no man. Or monarch. Or constitution. And the Audience now continues on Wednesday evenings, consigning the Tuesdays to distant history.

. . . and remains standing.

Churchill Your Majesty.

The year is 1952 and sitting opposite him is the twenty-five-year-old Queen.

Elizabeth Please . . . Prime Minister. . . . (*Indicating seat.*)

The Queen, as befits the protocol, is in mourning, and still wearing black. We are in the period of time after her father George VI's death, before her Coronation.
When she speaks, we notice the voice is quieter. More uncertain. Thinner. Higher. That of a girl.

I've ordered tea. Or would you prefer water?

Churchill stares in horror: 'Water?'

Something stronger, perhaps?

Churchill Oh, dear. Did no one explain? The Sovereign *never* offers a Prime Minister refreshment. Nor a chair. The precedent set by your great-great-grandmother was to keep us standing, like Privy Councillors. To waste time is a grievous sin. If there's one thing I have learned in fifty-two years of public service it is that there is no problem so complex nor crisis so grave that it cannot satisfactorily be resolved within twenty minutes. That was certainly also your dear father's view. Headlines only. No chat. So – in respect to his memory, shall we make a start?

Elizabeth Please.

The Queen reaches for something.

Churchill Second drawer. On the right.

Elizabeth What?

Churchill The notepad. Your father always took notes as I spoke.

Elizabeth I wasn't looking for a notepad. I was going to get my box.

The Queen bends down, picks up the Sovereign's red box.

I'm sure you can imagine, most of my time since the funeral has been taken up with our move to Buckingham Palace – but I have now had the chance to read the boxes. And I have the following questions. Can you give me a date for the end of rationing of sugar, butter and meat? What more can you tell me about our development of nuclear weapons? And do you envisage a military engagement, by UN forces, against China – in support of their allies in Korea?

Churchill No, no, stop! Goodness. Your Majesty . . . (*A patronising laugh.*) Did your father not tell you how these sessions work?

Elizabeth Yes. No. This is my first.

Churchill It's quite simple. The Prime Minister – that's me – comes to the Palace every Tuesday evening and explains what of note has transpired that past week in Cabinet, Parliament and Foreign Affairs. He then gives a brief indication of what is *going* to happen the following week. Throughout this the Sovereign – long may it be you – *listens*, makes notes, encourages and asks questions, maybe on the *rare* occasion expresses an opinion, then the Prime Minister goes. That is how it is, that is also how it reflects – in microcosm – how a constitutional monarchy works. The unchecked flow of information from one institution to the next. There is no finer system in the world.

Elizabeth I can see why you think that. You get to do all the talking. I get to take notes.

Churchill It's true. The British constitution, at first sight, *is* a little odd. But that's why it works so well. It's like a great ancient city – that's grown and evolved with time – organic and mutant, full of cul-de-sacs and short cuts, blind alleys, contradictions and follies. No planners could have come up with it. And at the heart of it, wrapped in a knot of mysteries and inconsistencies, is the relationship between you and me, Crown and Government.

Elizabeth The mystery being how *you* got so much power and I, as Head of State, get none. Wasn't it Gladstone who compared the British Prime Minister to a dictator? He was right.

Churchill Yes, but remember this dictator is still a human being. Ambitious. Grasping. Venal. That's how he got into office. And what ambitious, self-regarding dictator could fail to be impressed by all this? (*Gestures to their surroundings.*) By *you*? (*Gestures to the Queen.*) To a man they will be rendered speechless. Weak-kneed. And in that moment – the dictator will be yours to shape and to steer. One by one your Prime Ministers will fall under your spell. In here. In this audience. In this room.

Elizabeth Are you weak-kneed now, Mr Churchill?

Churchill (*smitten*) Oh, I am, Ma'am.

Elizabeth I meant literally. Would you like to sit?

Churchill (*proud*) Certainly not. I would not dream of it. Who knows where things would end?

He straightens to his full height, but in so doing he injures himself, and flinches again in pain.

Elizabeth They may actually end in your comfort. Please . . . ignore my great-great-grandmother and sit.

Churchill finally relents, and gratefully sits.

Let it be written into our unwritten constitution that from now on the audience will always be conducted this way. Now I have a question for you. My Coronation. I've heard you wish to postpone it until June next year. Why?

Churchill For your benefit entirely.

Elizabeth *My* benefit?

Churchill A long period between accession and Coronation was of great value to your father –

Elizabeth He had five months. You're proposing I have *sixteen*.

Churchill There is never enough time. Especially now, with this dreadful business of televising it. A quite unjustifiable vulgarisation . . . (*Stretching.*) Cables will have to be laid, angles worked out . . .

Elizabeth I know I'm young and have led a sheltered life, but that does not make me a fool. The delay is for *your* benefit.

Churchill Mine . . . ?

Elizabeth Your party wants you to resign and make way for Mr Eden. They think your clinging on to power is hurting the party and hurting the country. They even came to see my father hoping he'd talk you into stepping down – but his sudden death robbed him of the opportunity. You know no one would bring up your resignation while you were actively engaged in planning the Coronation. So by delaying my investiture, you are in fact hanging on to power. Is that true?

A beat.

A simple 'Yes' would suffice.

Churchill Ye–es, Ma'am.

Elizabeth In which case, I would suggest therefore that you are somewhat in *my* debt. So *if* I agree to the delay, perhaps you would consider returning the favour – quid pro quo – and supporting me on another matter.

Churchill Name it.

Elizabeth My husband, the Duke of Edinburgh. It is his wish, and mine, that I and our children take his name. Mountbatten.

Churchill looks up.

Churchill Is this Lord Mountbatten's idea? That man's ambitions know no bounds.

Elizabeth What is your answer?

Churchill No, Ma'am. You must not. It would be a grave mistake.

Elizabeth Why? For a wife to take her husband's name is the law of this country, is it not?

Churchill It is the custom, not the law.

Elizabeth Can the custom not apply to me, too?

Churchill Mountbatten was the adoptive name your husband took when he became a British citizen. His real name, you'll hardly need reminding, was Schleswig-Holstein-Sonderburg-Glücksburg of the Royal Houses of Denmark and Norway, and latterly of Greece. A convention of genealogists couldn't pinpoint that man's roots. Your grandfather already changed his name from Saxe-Coburg-Gotha to Windsor to spare his subjects the embarrassment of appearing to be ruled by the very people we were at war with. Mountbatten *itself* is an anglicisation of Battenburg. (*Exasperated.*) Just how many foreigners can we *have* in our royal family?

Elizabeth Then I suggest as a compromise the name of Edinburgh.

Churchill Ma'am. I beg you. That was a bestowed title.

Elizabeth All right. Edinburgh-Windsor.

Churchill Out of the question.

Elizabeth Why?

Churchill It's double-barrelled.

Elizabeth So?

Churchill It's common.

Elizabeth Prime Minister, I fear you're not taking me seriously. I am Queen of England but also a woman. And wife. To a man whose pride and whose strength are in part what attracted me to him. I want to be in a successful marriage. I would argue that stability under this roof might even be in the national interest. Had you considered *that*? So how do we do it? Tell me. How do we make our marriage work? If the man in this house is effectively neutered.

Churchill He knew what he was getting into.

Elizabeth He fell in love with me before he knew what he was getting into.

Churchill He was a citizen of no country. With no home of his own. England has given him both. *He* is fortunate, as are you. The duty which has befallen you both is the greatest honour on earth.

Elizabeth I might struggle, on occasion, with that honour.

Churchill Just never show that, Ma'am. It's not what your subjects want from you.

Elizabeth And is that *so* important? What my subjects want from me?

Churchill Yes. Even if we have no idea what that is.

Churchill looks at his watch.

Now we have overrun. Until next Tuesday.

He gets to his feet, bows deeply, and goes.

The Queen is left alone. Suddenly feeling the full weight and burden of her destiny. Shaken by the conversation.
A Dresser comes on, and starts dressing the Queen, changing her outfit. Presently, a voice.

Young Elizabeth I don't like this place.

A little eleven-year-old-girl walks on stage.

Elizabeth I know you don't.

The Young Elizabeth joins the Queen as she is being dressed by the window.

Young Elizabeth It's like being trapped in a museum. The rooms are cold. The corridors are dark. At night the wind moans in the chimneys. Like a thousand ghosts. (*A beat.*) I miss our old home.

Elizabeth I know you do.

Young Elizabeth We had neighbours then. This place has no neighbours. Just lots of people scurrying about doing funny jobs. (*Thinks.*) Like the Mistress of the Robes. The Yeoman of the Cellars.

Elizabeth The Keeper of the Privy Purse.

Young Elizabeth The Fendersmith. The Vermin-Catcher!

Elizabeth Ah, but you like him.

Young Elizabeth It's true. At least he smiles. Probably because there are so many mice for him to kill.

Elizabeth And you like the lake in the garden?

Young Elizabeth I do.

Elizabeth And the summer house?

Young Elizabeth I do.

Elizabeth And the roly-down hill at the end?

Young Elizabeth Yes, from which you can see the tops of the automobiles tearing down Buckingham Palace Road.

A silence.

I also like this particular window. It has the best aspect.

Elizabeth (*to herself*) There's a word I'd forgotten.

Young Elizabeth Look . . .

Elizabeth I'm looking.

Young Elizabeth The people outside all seem so busy. I can't help wondering what they are doing, where they're going, what they're all thinking of.

*They stare for a while, then Young Elizabeth sees
something, and pushes her older self away.*

Careful! Get back!

Elizabeth What?

Young Elizabeth One of them was looking up.

Young Elizabeth leans round the corner.

I don't want them to see me.

Elizabeth Why not? Everyone knows you live here.
They've seen you on the balcony. With Mummy and
Papa.

Young Elizabeth But that's me as . . . the other person.
This is me as . . . me.

*The Dresser finishes her work, then exits. The Queen
has become an older woman.*

Behind them, the door opens, and an Equerry appears.

Equerry The Prime Minister, Ma'am.

*The Queen lets the curtain drop, turns, and walks
back into to find the silhouette of a squat man in his
late forties in the doorway.*
    *It's Harold Wilson. He wears a Polaroid camera
around his neck.*

Wilson I suppose I should kick things off with an apology.

Elizabeth Whatever for?

Wilson Winning.

*It's 20 October 1964. Labour has just won the
General Election – by four seats.*

I'm aware of your affection for my predecessor.
Doubtless you would have preferred him to continue in
office, but the country said otherwise.

Elizabeth It is my duty *not* to have preferences.

Wilson We all do, though, don't we? We can't help it. It's human nature. And I can see the attraction of someone like 'Posh Alec'.

Elizabeth The Earl of Home.

Wilson Someone you can chat with about the racing. Someone well bred. High born. Who knows how to hold his cutlery. As opposed to a ruffian like me.

Elizabeth Hardly.

Wilson Still, I know a look when I see one, and when I came to the Palace to clock on – with Mary and the boys – don't think I didn't notice the looks on your courtiers' faces.

Elizabeth Did you see a look on *my* face?

Wilson No . . .

Elizabeth Well, then. It's just the wives and children are not generally invited to the kissing of hands.

Wilson Why? Did they get in the way?

Elizabeth No.

Wilson Did they make a mess? Or an unwelcome noise?

Elizabeth Of course not.

Wilson Well what's the problem, then? (*Indicates, turning through a circle.*) It's not like there was a lack of space.

Elizabeth The kissing of hands is a sober ritual, full of meaning and symbolism – where the Prime Minister takes the official oath, receives seals of office, and kisses hands in a symbol of fealty and loyalty, before being asked to form a government in his Sovereign's name . . .

Wilson It's also a jolly good day out if you happen to come from Huddersfield and your idea of a posh building is the public library.

Elizabeth I'm just saying it's not the custom.

Wilson 'Not done'. 'Not acceptable'. Don't bring your children.' 'Don't bring your wife.' '*Do* wear top hat and tails.' (*A beat.*) I don't even *own* a top hat and tails.

Elizabeth Whatever did you get married in?

Wilson A church.

Wilson stops, apologises.

Forgive my impertinence, Ma'am. I'm a simple man, intimidated by my surroundings.

Wilson hesitates.

My nerves are also an indication of the hopelessness of the situation.

Elizabeth Which situation?

Wilson The one I find myself in. Four seats! Whatever am I to do with a majority like that?

Elizabeth The danger of winning a protest vote is – you tend to inherit the mess which people have protested against.

Wilson And what a mess those Conservatives left us. What a diseased and poisoned appendix of a small and unrepresentative section of society. And what havoc they wreaked. Soaring land and house prices. Race riots. Sex scandals. Large-scale unemployment. Rejection from the EEC and an annual trade deficit of £800 million.

Elizabeth Yes, it's an unenviable legacy. What will you do about the balance of payments? Will you devalue?

Wilson No, Ma'am. A Labour Government devalued the pound once before with little success and my party cannot risk being seen as the 'party of devaluation'. (*A beat.*) It is also a matter of national pride. This is still a great country, and the pound is a powerful symbol.

Elizabeth Never underestimate the value of a symbol.

Wilson Especially one with one's face printed on it. (*A beat.*) Can't be an easy one to get used to.

Elizabeth What's that?

Wilson Having one's face on every coin and banknote.

Elizabeth No. I remember seeing my father's face on a shilling for the first time. And thinking how odd it looked. At the same time realising I would probably one day have to look at my own face. (*Quiet.*) But one never knows what destiny has in store for one. Did you ever imagine you'd be Prime Minister?

Wilson Goodness, no. There's a photograph of me taken outside Downing Street aged eight which some people interpreted as such. There was never a 'scheme' or 'plan'. No, half the children in Milnsbridge – where I grew up – never had any boots or shoes to their feet. They wore clogs, because clogs lasted longer. As children we never had ambitions or dreams beyond survival! I almost died of typhoid aged six. And now I'm here drinking tea with the Queen of England.

Elizabeth (*corrects*) United Kingdom . . .

Wilson As Leader of her Government.

Elizabeth Mrs Wilson must be very proud.

Wilson Oh, no. She's furious. She'd have been happiest staying at Oxford. As a young don's wife. She loved our life there. Doesn't care for the limelight. Or the cut and thrust of Westminster life. Certainly doesn't care for our new home.

Elizabeth Downing Street?

Wilson 'Living in the office', she calls it.

Elizabeth My husband feels the same way about this place. *Loathes* it. (*A beat.*) We *all* do, actually.

Wilson No!

Elizabeth Yes.

Wilson No!

Elizabeth Yes!

Wilson Goodness! Who else knows that?

Elizabeth No one. (*A meaningful look.*) And I hope no one ever will.

Wilson Actually, she's happiest in the Scilly Isles.

Elizabeth Oh. What do you have there?

Wilson A prefabricated bungalow. Three beds.

Elizabeth How lovely. And what do you like to do there?

Wilson Gardening. Walks. Taking boats to the other islands.

Elizabeth I love it on the water – away from it all. You know, it's the one place I can kick off my shoes, and walk barefoot.

Wilson On the water?

Elizabeth On the *Britannia*.

The Queen looks at her watch.

Well, if there's nothing else, I think we have done enough for today.

Wilson Ma'am?

Elizabeth That's all for now.

Wilson Is that it? A cosy chat about holiday homes, and a nice cup of tea . . .?

Elizabeth Our twenty minutes are up.

Wilson I make it sixteen.

Elizabeth Was there anything you felt you needed to add?

Wilson There was. If my manner earlier was a little abrupt, forgive me. I just want to impress upon Her Majesty the gravity of the situation. For too long now the assumption has prevailed that the Empire still exists, and all will be well – because it always has been in the past. It's not true. There's a revolution taking place out there, and the old ruling class is sleepwalking right through it, looking backwards when everyone else is looking forward. The fact is there *is* no ruling class any more. Just one nation. That can be just as great, but will never be the same.

The Queen gets up, indicating that the time is up.

Wilson Now if I could just . . .

Wilson produces a camera. The Equerry appears.

Wilson Mary insisted.

'Snap': a picture is taken. Wilson smiling proudly. Then his smile fades.

C'mon, Wilson . . .

He straightens, looks the Queen in the eye.

The picture's for me, Ma'am. This is the proudest moment of my life.

Elizabeth That's very kind.

Wilson smiles proudly as they pose.

Wilson If my colleagues on the left of the party could see me now. I'm afraid they despair of my monarchist leanings.

'Snap': another picture is taken.

One more, if you don't mind, Ma'am. For my father. James Herbert Wilson. He's not been well. Lumbago.

'Snap': another picture.

Until next week.

Elizabeth Prime Minister.

Wilson takes his camera, and bows deeply. Exaggeratedly deeply. Producing another bemused smile from the Queen.

The Queen exits the stage as Young Elizabeth walks on with her Scottish nanny, Bobo Macdonald.

Young Elizabeth What did Mummy mean tonight when she said everything would be different?

Bobo It means as of today your father will not just be your father. He will be your king, too. And that's how you'll have to refer to him. In public.

Young Elizabeth Can't I still call him Papa?

Bobo Maybe. But don't be surprised if he says it has to be 'Sir'. It also means you'll have to curtsy to him whenever you greet him, or say goodbye . . .

Young Elizabeth And Mummy?

Bobo To her, too.

Young Elizabeth That's silly. I'll get the giggles.

Bobo You mustn't do that. You wouldn't like it if people giggled when they curtsy to you.

Young Elizabeth Why would they do that?

Bobo Because that's what you do to the heiress presumptive. And call you 'Ma'am'. Your friends, too.

Young Elizabeth What if I don't want them to? Please, don't make them do that. They'll hate me. How can we stop this?

Bobo We can't. Unless your mother and father –

She checks herself.

– the King and Queen have a boy.

The Queen enters. She is now eighty-three years old, white-haired and showing the first signs of frailty.

Bobo Now what's it going to be? Am I going to tell you a bedtime story? Or are we going to say our prayers?

Young Elizabeth Prayers.

Bobo And what are we going to pray for?

Young Elizabeth That the King and Queen have a boy.

A lighting change. Bobo and Young Elizabeth exit.

Brown So *humiliating.*

Enter Gordon Brown, fifty-eight, the Queen's eleventh Prime Minister. It's late September 2009.

Five attempts, Ma'am, *five* to secure private bilateral talks with President Obama, and he refused point blank . . . yet proceeded to have one-on-ones with everyone else right under my nose. The Dutch, for God's sake. Finally, after repeated representations by my ambassador –

Elizabeth (*under her breath*) *My* ambassador.

Brown – he agreed to a meeting in the kitchens. For five minutes. For what his aides insultingly called a 'walk and talk'.

Elizabeth In the kitchens?

Brown *Through* the kitchens. Of the United Nations building. A short cut taken by his security people. The Head of Her Majesty's Government. America's staunchest ally, a political brotherhood forged over two centuries, gets fifty yards by the refrigerators. Couldn't have been more insulting.

Elizabeth I'm touched by your indignation. But I wouldn't read too much into it.

Brown How can I not? Everyone else is. Leader writers and bloggers taking it as an indication of the White House distancing itself from the candidate they fully expect to lose the next General Election. I suppose it serves me right. I probably will lose, and only have myself to blame. After all, you told me to go for it.

Elizabeth For what?

Brown A snap election. In 2007. When I was still in my honeymoon. To establish a personal mandate.

Elizabeth Ah, yes. I'm a great believer in displays of strength. When Mr Major told me he intended to face down his rebels in 1995 . . .

Brown 'Back me or sack me.' I remember.

Elizabeth I didn't discourage him. Nor Mr Wilson in 1974, when he had a minority Labour government.

Brown *All* of us politicians could learn a thing or two from you. We're *all* in the survival business, and God knows, if anyone has pulled off an inexplicable survival against the odds it's you . . . I mean this institu— I mean . . . Oh . . .

Brown tails off, checks himself.

Elizabeth I think that started life as a compliment – but ended up somewhere else.

The Queen smiles.

It's true. From a purely logical perspective our 'inexplicable' survival on the throne is perhaps hard to justify. But that's where one's grateful for one's faith and the clarity that brings.

Brown (*not following*) Ma'am . . .?

Elizabeth The Coronation is no civic event. It's a consecration that takes place in God's house. Under *His* roof.

Brown stares. Still not understanding.

It's *His* will that we are where we are.

A silence.

Back to your trip?

Brown Well, after a couple more days in Pittsburgh, and a productive meeting with Colonel Gaddafi.

Elizabeth Was he in his tent? With all his female bodyguards?

Brown Not this time. I met him in New York. At the UN. In which he reiterated his commitment to abandoning his weapons programme and his desire to continue investing in the UK. I came home.

Elizabeth I heard he'd taken to referring to himself both as 'Leader of the Revolution' and the 'King of Kings'. Which seems to be wanting to have it both ways. (*A beat.*) Did you at least manage to get away for the weekend?

Brown I did. And even found some time to think about a book I'm planning to write. About the financial crisis engulfing us all. And how the world can work together to best prevent another one in the future; through coordinated monetary policy and regulation . . . by way of some post-Keynesian stuff about insufficient aggregate demands . . .

Elizabeth That was your *weekend*?

Brown Yes, Ma'am.

Elizabeth No guests then?

Brown Oh, yes. Someone from the Department of International Development whose name escapes me, someone from Save the Children – a corpulent woman. But Sarah took care of them. Gave them the tour.

Elizabeth Swimming in the indoor pool? A walk in the woods?

Brown You know the Chequers routine.

Elizabeth We have a similar one at Balmoral as you know. Picnics by the lake, walks on the moors after lunch . . .

Brown Weather permitting.

Elizabeth Excuse me. No *matter* the weather.

Brown smiles.

Brown I shall never forget the story you told about my predecessor turning up at Balmoral in brand new country clothes.

Elizabeth Mr Blair? Yes. He and his lady wife, Cheryl . . .

Brown Che-*rie*.

Elizabeth In spanking new tweed . . . I *think* with all the price tags still attached. We were all very amused.

Brown (*erupting in joy*) Ha!

Brown slaps his thigh. His laughter is alarmingly loud and without restraint. The Queen is startled.

Elizabeth Goodness.

Brown Forgive me – but jokes at his expense never fail to cheer me up.

Elizabeth That's a *Schadenfreude* you have in common with all your predecessors.

Brown No, Ma'am. Trust me. This one is in a league of its own.

Elizabeth Worse than Eden and Churchill? I doubt that. Than Heath and Thatcher?

Brown You'd be surprised.

Elizabeth I suppose he took a long time to go.

Brown Ten years. One month. Three weeks. Four days.

Elizabeth Churchill took even longer. Fifteen years until he made way as Conservative leader for poor Mr Eden.

Brown That's the first time I've heard the word 'poor' uttered in the same sentence as 'Eden'.

Elizabeth He was so dashing. One forgets that now. On the electoral trail in 1955 the women of Britain lined the streets. A year later, he was a disgraced man. I recall a conversation I had with him – (*She smiles as she remembers.*) I was in an evening gown – tiara and Garter sash, having been photographed by Cecil Beaton – which was almost word for word identical to one I had with Mr Blair almost fifty years later. The similarities, the parallels were striking . . . (*A beat.*) I suppose that's what happens if you stick round long enough. The same people, the same ideas come round again and again. Wearing a different coloured tie.

The Queen turns.

Elizabeth So, back to your weekend, and all this industriousness. Were you up very early?

Brown Four thirty.

Elizabeth Oh, dear.

Brown It's all right. I never sleep much.

Elizabeth Since when?

Brown Since always.

Elizabeth Harold Wilson always used to say, 'The main requirement of a Prime Minister is a good night's sleep . . . and a sense of history.' Mrs Thatcher taught herself to need very little towards the end. But I'm not sure how reassured I am by that. I like the idea of any person with the power to start nuclear war being rested. (*A beat.*) Besides, lack of sleep can have a knock-on effect in other areas.

Brown Such as?

Elizabeth One's general sense of health.

A silence.

And happiness.

A silence.

And equilibrium.

Brown looks up. A silence.

I gather there's been some concern . . .

Brown About what?

Elizabeth Your happiness. Don't worry. You wouldn't be the first in your position to feel overwhelmed. Despondent.

She searches for the right word.

Depressed.

Brown I'm fine. It's all been checked out. I can assure you.

A silence.

From a constitutional perspective you have nothing to worry about.

Silence.

They've given me some stuff to take. Means you put on a bit of weight, and I can't eat certain food.

He searches his pockets.

I've got the list somewhere. Cheese is a no-no, apparently. Caffeine, bean curd, alcohol, avocados, banana peel, pepperoni . . .

Elizabeth 'Always destined for the highest office. A giant dwarfing his contemporaries. Half Socrates, half George Washington.'

Brown Who's that?

Elizabeth It was how your former headmaster described *you*, Mr Brown. 'A Colossus'. (*A beat.*) 'With a little bit of OCD.'

A silence.

I have it, too, you know.

Brown What?

Elizabeth OCD. With shoes. And pens. All need to be in a row. Neat and tidy. (*A beat.*) Like soldiers.

Brown What happens if they're not?

Elizabeth I become 'vexed'.

Brown I have it with nails. Can't help biting them. And underlining.

Elizabeth What do you underline?

Brown *Everything.*

Elizabeth How very satisfying.

A silence.

Mental illness has been in my family for some time. The agitation and hallucinations which troubled George III were diagnosed to have recurred recently in Prince William of Gloucester. Queen Victoria had several lengthy bouts of depression – some argue after the death of her husband she never came out of it. People called it mourning, but it wasn't. Two of my mother's nieces, Nerissa and Katherine, were incarcerated in 1941 in the Royal Earlswood Asylum for Mental Defectives. (*Tailing off.*) In Redhill.

A silence.

First cousins.

A silence.

The elder was said to look remarkably like me.

A silence.

Brown It's the job I dreamt of my whole life, being Leader of the Labour Party. In government. But I must accept I may not be as well cut out for it as I'd hoped. I'm probably better suited as a academic. Tucked away –

Elizabeth 'Tucked away'. How lovely.

Brown – at one of the great Scottish Universities.

A silence.

Elizabeth The unlived lives within us all.

More silence.

In my unlived life, I'd be miles from anywhere, a house in the country. A farm, probably. Lots of children, lots of horses, lots of dogs. Everyone mucking in, being allowed to get grubby.

Brown Which part of the world?

Elizabeth Oh, Scotland. I was brought up by Scotswomen . . . and not just my mother. All the nannies, too. Good stout Scotswomen. One in particular, Bobo Macdonald, she slept in a room with me until I was fifteen – she was a wonderful storyteller. And would tell me stories at night about what it was like – on the outside.

She tails off.

But how did we get started on this? That fire is too hot. It's mid September, what were they thinking? If you don't mind I shall ask them to leave it unmade next week . . .

Brown I won't be here next week, Ma'am.

Elizabeth Oh?

Brown Party Conference.

Elizabeth Of course. Where are you this year?

Brown Brighton.

Elizabeth How lovely. (*Stops, thinks.*) Is it lovely?

Brown No, Ma'am. Too many Tories down there. I'd have preferred Blackpool. Good Labour heartland. A couple of marginal seats we could have cleaned up there, too. In the process. Lancaster and Fleetwood. Blackpool North and Cleveleys.

Elizabeth That would have been very efficient of you. How's the speech going?

Brown I've got a first draft. Which has come in a bit long.

Elizabeth Always a mistake to outstay one's welcome. I make sure the Christmas speech never goes beyond eight minutes. That's the limit of human endurance, I think.

Brown I'm afraid my lot'll have to put up with me a little longer than that.

Elizabeth Well, you can't say I didn't warn you.

Brown and the Queen walk off.

The Equerry walks on, and walks to a drinks cabinet.

Equerry If there's one thing Her Majesty really loathes, it's being ill. She is a great believer in fresh air and exercise as preventative measures, and *always* wears gloves on public rounds and studiously avoids people with coughs and sniffles. As a consequence, the occasions where she has called in sick over the past sixty years can be counted on one hand . . .

He is making a hot toddy.

The occasion in November 1971 comes to mind, when Her Majesty contracted chickenpox – a 'ridiculous disease', she called it. She resumed her duties the moment she was free of infection – including meeting Prime Minister Edward Heath for an audience, still covered in spots! And in December 1992, shortly after the publication of Andrew Morton's book about Diana, the Queen was struck by a *very* nasty cold.

And lights come up on the Queen in the Audience Room as the Equerry brings her a steaming LemSip. She is not in good health. She is running a fever and is in a filthy mood.

Equerry A hot lemon drink, Ma'am.

Elizabeth Thank you. Did you spice it up a bit?

Equerry I did.

Elizabeth One shot or two?

Equerry (*clears throat*) Three.

Elizabeth Good.

The Queen takes a sip.

Equerry The doctor *did* ask me to impress upon you that continued bed rest was advisable . . .

Elizabeth I'll be fine.

Equerry And that while running a fever, any exertion or unnecessary stress might tire you excessively . . .

Elizabeth Don't be silly.

Equerry Or prolong the illness . . .

Elizabeth I'll be fine. It's just a cold.

Equerry (*correcting*) Flu, Ma'am.

Elizabeth Cold.

Equerry The doctor was quite clear . . .

Elizabeth (*barks, suddenly furious*) It's a *cold*! Now *scram*!

The Equerry and several dogs scatter.

John Major appears in the doorway. He bows from the neck.

Elizabeth I do hope you bring good news. I could do with cheering up.

Major senses her mood. And freezes.

Major I . . . I'm afraid not.

37

He takes a deep breath. This won't be easy. Unsure where to begin:

It was a probably a mistake my embarking on this whole thing, and imagining I could make a difference. I just thought having successfully negotiated safe havens for the Kurds that my mediating skills would help reach a breakthrough here . . . (*A beat.*) But it seems nothing could have prepared me for the factionalism at Kensington Palace.

Elizabeth Who did you see first?

Major The Prince of Wales.

The Queen perceptibly stiffens. The merest mention of her son irritates her.

Major It's clear he feels very angry and betrayed following the unfortunate business with the Gilbey tapes . . . and that there is now little warmth or respect left for the Princess of Wales. Worse, he feels she is becoming increasingly problematic, and concern is growing about her influence over the Princes.

Thunderclouds pass over the Queen's brow. Her knuckles momentarily appear to whiten.

Elizabeth And the Princess of Wales?

Major I'm sad to report she appeared quite fragile. She feels the marriage is to blame for her depression and several suicide attempts. She continues to find the Prince of Wales uncaring, cold, and is hurt by the fact that he persists in treating her like the eighteen-year-old she was when they got engaged. When I urged her to be more compassionate and try to see it from *his* perspective, too – a conflict-resolution technique I picked up shuttling between rival Serbian, Croat and ethnic Albanian warlords at the Geneva conference on Bosnia this year –

she said that in a sense they'd *both* been victims since he'd obviously had feelings for someone else all along, and they had both been pressurised into an 'appropriate' marriage by the Royal Fam—

Silence. Major tails off.

Elizabeth Ah, so it's my fault?

Major She never went that far, Ma'am. Never *once* referred to you personally. Or the Queen Mother.

Elizabeth Just the institution we represent.

Major (*clears throat*) She did offer some thoughts on that.

Elizabeth May I hear them?

Major I don't think it will help.

Elizabeth I didn't suggest it would *help*. I asked to hear them.

Major All right . . . (*Clears throat.*) The Princess felt the monarchy in its current form was outdated, unegalitarian and unrepresentative of the modern country Britain has become – and that the people were growing sick of it. She mentioned the fact that most monarchies in western democracies had been swept away by now – Portugal for example, Italy, Greece . . .

Elizabeth That we should be swept away, too?

Major She didn't go that far, but I think she feels – and here the Government would tend to agree –

A silence. Major gathers the courage.

– that there might be a case to be made for *further* reform and modernisation . . . (*A beat.*) On top of the extremely generous concessions you already made this year when you agreed to foot the bill for the repair to your own home, Windsor Castle, after the fire.

Stony silence.
  Major clears throat.

It's just when you agreed to those measures, we expected
public approval to be reflected in the polls, and it seems it
hasn't yet – the most recent one suggesting . . . that every
second Briton now considers you – the monarchy – a
luxury the country cannot afford.

  The Queen looks away.

So there are one or two further *tiny* modifications – the
payment of inheritance tax for example – which the
Government would ask Her Majesty to consider just to
get things back where they belong . . . approval-wise.

Elizabeth If the Crown pays inheritance tax, that makes
us like everyone else. And we're *not* like everyone else.
That's the point of us.

Major Very well. Opening up Buckingham Palace.

Elizabeth To what?

Major People.

Elizabeth *People?*

Major It would give them a chance to share in the legacy.
Make them feel like they know you.

Elizabeth I don't *wish* to be known.

Major All right. And *Britannia*. The Royal Yacht.

Elizabeth What about it? You don't want people
traipsing round *her* too?

Major No.

  He braces himself, then:

I'm suggesting she's taken out of service.

Elizabeth (*quiet*) Never!

Major I'm aware this is a sensitive matter . . .

Elizabeth That yacht means everything to me. She was launched the year I was crowned. She's been the one constant in my life. Commissioned by my father.

Major These are difficult times economically.

Elizabeth Forty thousand miles I travelled on *one tour alone* – in service to this country. Five American Presidents have stayed aboard her. She has taken us to the remotest corners, and helped hold together the Commonwealth. That yacht is my refuge. The one place I feel at home.

Major But the costs . . .

Elizabeth What costs?

Major Two hundred and sixty sailors, most of them permanent, two dozen bandsmen, red boxes being helicoptered out every day from London at great expense . . .

Elizabeth Have you ever set foot *inside* of her?

Major No.

Elizabeth When you do, I suggest the one thing that will strike you will be her modesty. (*Rising indignation.*) Enough now. Enough. This family gives every minute of every day in service to the British people and do you see me complain? Never. Serving this country is my duty and my privilege. But every now and then I must be allowed to draw the line. I am the Crown, after all . . .

Major Yes, Ma'am.

The Equerry enters, having heard raised voices.

Elizabeth You'd do well to reflect on that – on *who* I am and *how* I got here. It's *God's will*, understand?

Equerry Running a temperature, Ma'am.

Elizabeth (*raising voice*) And *He's* not telling us to give up *Britannia*.

Equerry Open wide . . .

The Equerry delicately puts the thermometer in the Queen's mouth in an attempt to silence her.

I'm sorry, Prime Minister, we must leave it there.

Major Of course.

He politely gets to his feet, excusing himself.

Elizabeth Make up your minds what you *all* want from us!! That's all we ask!

Major goes.

(*Calling after him*) Just make up your minds!!

The Equerry soothes her.

Equerry Nice and still for one minute.

Elizabeth (*snaps*) Oh, for goodness sake.

The Equerry goes. Young Elizabeth walks on. The Queen looks up, and double-takes.

(*Speaking through thermometer.*) What *have* you done?

It's a shocking sight. Young Elizabeth is covered in dark liquid. Her hair is matted.

Young Elizabeth I poured ink over my head.

Elizabeth Why?

Young Elizabeth She's just so awful. I wanted her *out*.

Elizabeth Who?

Young Elizabeth The French Mademoiselle.

Elizabeth What did she do?

Young Elizabeth Made me copy things out again and again. Like a slave. And shouted at me. I complained about her to Mummy, but she didn't listen. So I did this. And screamed. (*A beat.*) You know, my piercing scream?

Elizabeth I know the one.

Young Elizabeth I kept it up for half an hour. Getting louder and louder. And it worked. She's run away.

Elizabeth What happens if the next one isn't nice?

Young Elizabeth I'll get rid of her, too.

Elizabeth Good for you.

Her expression toughens.

Sometimes one just has to draw the line.

Blackout.

End of Act One.

Act Two

The Equerry walks out on an empty, darkened stage.

Equerry Every August the Prime Minister is invited to
Scotland to spend a weekend as a guest at Balmoral
Castle. While there, Her Majesty and the PM often take
a moment to catch up on matters of State. Generally they
meet in the drawing room.

The Equerry turns to face the dark space behind him.

A desk in the corner, made by George Hepplewhite in
1775. Two Landseer portraits. A trophy of a stag's head,
a fourteen-pointer, believed to have been shot by Prince
Albert in 1844. On the mantelpiece a gold-framed clock
made by Ferdinand Berthoud. Two chairs, from Arbuckle
and Haines, in Inverurie, with a tartan throw hand-woven
by Mrs Janet MacDuff, an estate employee. A large
fireplace dominates the room, but supplementary warmth
is provided, when required, by a three-bar electric heater
bought from John Lewis on the 5th of August 1968.

A lighting change:
   *It's six p.m. on 20th August 1968. We're in a
drawing room at Balmoral Castle, Aberdeenshire.
Wooden panelling. Stag's antlers. Tartan carpets.*
   *From outside the windows we can clearly hear the
rain falling.*
   *A uniformed Major of the Argyll and Sutherland
Highlanders serenades his sovereign in the distance.*
   *Harold Wilson staggers in. Soaking wet and
shivering. He is wearing ill-fitting country clothes.
A drowned rat.*

Equerry Prime Minister!

Wilson M-m-may I stand by the fire? Just a moment.

He stands by the three-bar electric fire. The Queen enters, wearing tartan.

Elizabeth You got caught in the 'rude rain'! It's what the locals call it.

Wilson That's not rain, Ma'am. It's daggers of merciless ice. Blowing at fifty miles per hour. H-h-horizontally. In August. This unholy mess –

He indicates his utterly dishevelled appearance.

– is as a result of me popping fifty yards to the car to fetch Mary's reading glasses . . .

Elizabeth (*chuckles*) The Tsar of Russia – when he came to visit – claimed it was colder here than in the wastes of Siberia.

Wilson thaws by the fire, drying off.

Be reassured. I've spoken to the ghillies and told them we'll have our picnic at Gelder Shiel. It's covered there.

Wilson Picnic? Good God . . .

His face perceptibly falls.

I was told that in the event of bad weather we'd be having dinner here in the Castle.

Elizabeth But this *isn't* bad weather. Just a spot of summer rain. How did you enjoy the Games today?

Wilson walks over to take a seat.

Wilson The enjoyment of any sport comes with an understanding of its subtleties. I am sure there *are* nuances to caber tossing, putting the stone, and tugs of war, and profound allegorical significance to Highland dancing, but I'm afraid they are lost on me.

Elizabeth It's quite simple. The sports are trials of strength going back to the days of clan military recruitments, and the Highland dancers –

The Queen lifts her arms above her head in a lyre shape, spreading her fingers and pointing a toe.

– symbolise magnificent stags, leading their herds.

The hands above her head, it becomes apparent, represent antlers. From outside the bagpipe music strikes up again.

Wilson Here we go again. (*Indicating the window.*) Will that chappie never stop?

Elizabeth The Piper to the Sovereign plays every morning at nine a.m., wherever the Crown is in the world. Has done ever since Queen Victoria. One just retired, so we're auditioning for his replacement. This one's rather good, I think.

The Queen goes to look out of the window. We notice she is wearing a tartan skirt.

Wilson Honestly, you lot and your 'Scottishness'. Doesn't fool me for a second. You should have someone playing the accordion in lederhosen. This whole place looks like a Rheinland schloss. Come to think of it, it *is* a Rheinland schloss.

Elizabeth It was built by a local Aberdeen architect, with stone from our quarries, with just one or two modifications to the design by Prince Albert.

Wilson I can guess how that went . . . (*Mimicking Prince Albert's German accent.*) 'Please make it look exactly like a Rheinland schloss.'

The Queen can't help laughing.

Do you mind if I smoke, Ma'am?

Elizabeth Not at all.

Wilson produces a cigar, and lights it.

Have you mislaid your pipe?

Wilson No. The pipe's strictly for the television and the campaign trail. All that folksy unpacking of tobacco and paraphernalia makes me approachable, and buys me time if the question's a tricky one. The cigar's my first love, but too potent a symbol of capitalist privilege and power. If I walked round puffing one of these I'd lose the left in my party in a second.

Elizabeth The impression I get is you already have. By reneging on all those radical election promises you made.

Wilson Maybe I'll gain new friends on the right.

Elizabeth No. *They* hate you for devaluing the pound. And that after all that grandstanding, and promises not to . . . (*Mimics.*) 'My party will not be seen as the party of devaluation.'

Wilson All right, all right. I thought we were on holiday.

Elizabeth We are.

Wilson Then couldn't we leave politics out of it? Just for twenty-four hours? I've come here to recover. Get my strength back.

Elizabeth Holiday it is. Can I offer you a drink?

Wilson I thought you'd never ask.

Elizabeth Whisky?

Wilson Brandy, Ma'am.

The Queen pours him a drink.

There is a curious paradox at the heart of political life. All politicians crave being loved – what is an election if not a popularity contest? But the first requirement of the job is to be hated.

Elizabeth Mine, too, incidentally. We're both lightning rods, Prime Minister. Pressure valves. People need someone to be angry with, and generally that's us. But you won't catch me complaining about it.

Wilson I wasn't complaining.

Elizabeth Yes, you were. I heard it in your voice.

Wilson No, what you heard, Ma'am, was the sound of a heart breaking. Dreams shattering. When you realise you have not *won* an election at all, it is the previous government that has *lost* it . . .

Elizabeth Would you like me to cheer you up?

Wilson Please!

Elizabeth That is something of which your nemesis, Mr Heath, has no idea. He still thinks he might actually *win* against you.

Wilson Ha! The Grocer? Don't mention his name to me. That man is odious. Odious I tell you. Even my saintly wife Mary, not a malicious thought in her head, cannot bear him. The man's incompetent, insensitive and, worst of all, he's a snob.

Elizabeth And what makes you think I'm not?

Wilson I've been in professional politics twenty-seven years, and I pride myself on this: I can sniff a Tory at a hundred paces. And you're not one, Ma'am. Not a real one, anyway. You understand ordinary people. Working people. And where can that come from? Having been locked up in mausoleums like this all your life. You may be the richest woman in the world, but you're also worrying about the cost of the central heating, telling yourself to go back into the room and switch the lights off –

Elizabeth (*to herself*) It's the Bobo in me.

Wilson Deep down you're not just happier with normal folk, you're one of us. I'd even go as far to say –

He looks left and right.

There's a good Labour woman in there somewhere.

The Queen laughs.

Elizabeth If I were Labour, I would approve of your proposals to reform the House of Lords.

Wilson And you don't?

Elizabeth Certainly not. And I'm not the only one. I read the *Mail* which suggested the proposed two tiers of the new House of Lords was –

Wilson I know – (*Reciting perfectly.*) 'A confusing hodge-podge of antithetical ideas and policies, a situation of needless bureaucracy where deposed hereditary peers will inevitably reclaim their voting rights when they are selected as one of the eighty-five new life peers.'

He shrugs.

What are you doing reading that rag? They got their facts wrong for a start. It's eighty life peers we would create. And that bit at the bottom of the third paragraph about my proposals being 'a step towards an atheistic society with no moral rudder'? I'm keeping sixteen bishops! What more do they want? (*Under his breath.*) Still sixteen too many as far as I'm concerned.

Elizabeth Goodness. You certainly took it to heart.

Wilson No, Ma'am. I just read it.

Elizabeth But clearly often enough to memorise it.

Wilson I'm afraid that's something that comes naturally. (*Taps head.*) To be honest, I don't know how anyone could do the job without it.

Elizabeth I don't understand.

Wilson 3.1415926535897932384664338327950288419 716939937510582097494459230 . . .

Elizabeth What on earth is that?

Wilson Pi. To 66 places. Would you like me to go on? I can do 135.

Elizabeth You have a photographic memory?

Wilson I do.

Elizabeth You memorised the article having read it –

Wilson Skimmed it. Once. Over a boiled egg.

Elizabeth I don't believe you.

Wilson Yes.

Elizabeth No!

Wilson Yes. Go on. Test me, then.

The Queen looks up.

Open up a book. Any book. On any page.

Elizabeth A book . . . ?

The Queen looks around the study. No sign of a book anywhere. Embarrassed, she walks over to her desk. Picks up the phone.

Hello. Could you bring us a book. (*Listens.*) It doesn't matter what kind. (*Listens.*) There must be one somewhere. (*Listens.*) Ask someone from the household to go into one of the empty guest rooms. Try the Green Bedroom. In the East Wing.

She hangs up. A silence. Wilson puffs his cigar. The Queen sips her Dubonnet.

Won't be a moment.

Wilson Yes, it will. It's a journey of about three miles. In a private house. It's a scandal. Took me an hour to walk to breakfast this morning.

Elizabeth You love it.

Presently, approaching footsteps. A breathless member of staff comes in holding a book. He passes it to Wilson.

Thank you.

Wilson looks at the hardback book.

(*Reading.*) *Life in a Crack Regiment: A Novel of German Military Manners and Morals* by Baron von Schlicht

He raises his eyebrow. The Queen clears her throat.

The Duke of Edinburgh's sister was here last week.

Wilson Pick a page.

He passes the book to the Queen, she picks a page, then passes it back. Wilson scans it briefly, then, giving her the book to check:

'The final German victory over England is only a question of time. Before long we will have air superiority and 90,000 men, horses and tanks will rise out of the sea and on to British soil. Once we have established dominance, we will begin occupation. Key targets will be neutralised – the Prime Minister, Marxists, Freemasons,

Jews, all confirmed enemies of Germany . . . with the
exception of –'

Wilson looks up, indicates to the Queen.

Elizabeth (*heart sinks*) '– the British Royal Family . . .
who we believe are deeply sympathetic.'

*The Queen clears her throat. Puts down the book,
anxious to change the subject.*

Bravo, Prime Minister. Now, we must leave for the
picnic.

Wilson Oh, joy.

Elizabeth Don't be like that. It's a rare occasion where
you'll be together with friends. Who don't *hate* you. You
might even enjoy it. It's a beautiful summer's evening.
Years of city living and high office have made you soft.

They walk towards the door.

I thought you wore wooden shoes to school in Halifax?

Wilson Huddersfield. Not me personally, Ma'am. Some
of the other boys.

Elizabeth Ah, so the hardship was someone else's?
Typical politician. (*Opening the door.*) Now, enough of
your clogs. Where are my dogs . . .?

*The Queen and Wilson walk out. The Queen calls out
to several dogs.*
    *Wilson stops, then pops his head back into the
drawing room, and –*
    'Click': turns the light out.
    Blackout.

*Fade in: suspenseful, grave music. A distinct change of
mood. Scene change.*
    *It's 30th October 1956. We are now in the King's
Corridor. The atmosphere is tense. Anxious.*

A tall man enters. Anthony Eden, fifty-nine, Conservative, the Queen's second Prime Minister.

Eden's hair is grey, he appears somewhat agitated, but there are still flashes, shards, of the matinee-idol looks and aristocratic bearing that helped him to high office.

Equerry Not long now, Prime Minister. Her Majesty will be with you shortly.

Eden Thank you.

An awkward silence.

May I have a glass of water?

The Equerry goes to tell a Footman to bring water.
Eden uses the moment with the Equerry's back being turned to take some pills.

He does not sit down. He is too restless, too agitated. He paces around, checking his watch; the ravages of extreme stress and lack of sleep.

(*Irritable.*) Will she be very much longer?

Equerry The urgency of the situation has been conveyed to Her Majesty, but she had a long-standing commitment with Mr Beaton . . .

Eden Who?

Equerry The photographer. (*A beat.*) And he generally runs late.

At that moment, Eden's Private Secretary walks on.

Private Secretary This just came through, sir.

Eden impatiently opens the telegram, hoping for good news. His reaction, reading it:

Eden Oh, Christ.

*Presently the door opens to reveal the Queen. Thirty
years old. Spectacular – in full ballgown, tiara, etc.
   And Cecil Beaton, who packs up his equipment,
and bows as he leaves.*

Elizabeth Prime Minister.

Eden Your Majesty.

Elizabeth I'm sorry to have kept you waiting.

Eden Events are unfolding at great speed. Would Her
Majesty like me to walk her through it?

Elizabeth Please.

Eden Yesterday morning, the Israeli Army launched an
attack into Egyptian territory, the Sinai Peninsula, and is
rapidly approaching the Suez Canal. The Egyptian army
has mobilised a retaliatory force and is about to engage.
Her Majesty's Government has now made two separate
and simultaneous appeals to the Egyptians and Israelis to
halt all acts of war and to allow Anglo-French forces into
the country to preserve the peace and the freedom of
passage for all vessels in the Suez Canal. The Israelis have
expressed a willingness to comply if the Egyptians do, but
sadly, President Nasser has refused thus far.

Elizabeth When does the deadline expire?

Eden Tomorrow morning, Ma'am.

Elizabeth And the next step, in your view, would be?

Eden Military intervention, Ma'am.

Elizabeth War?

Eden Indeed. To keep the peace. It's the correct thing to
do, Ma'am. The man's an Asiatic fascist, and I think we
all remember too well what the cost can be of giving in to
fascism.

Elizabeth The view of the Joint Intelligence Committee report from April this year was more balanced, suggesting we should view him as a 'successful revolutionary'.

Eden Don't be fooled. Seizing the Suez Canal was a deliberate act of nationalist aggression.

Elizabeth Which arguably we provoked.

Eden A French and English company owned that canal.

Elizabeth But it was built by Egyptians. And one hundred and twenty thousand of them died doing so.

Eden Nasser's claim. You can't believe that!

Elizabeth Still, even if it were half that number . . .

Eden The Suez Canal is a vital artery of the Commonwealth, the only route by which we get our oil. I should mention we also have a significant number of British and French nationals in Egypt we need to protect.

Elizabeth How many?

Eden Three thousand.

Elizabeth And how many servicemen are you proposing to send?

Eden Forty-five thousand.

You could hear a pin drop.

But no troops on the ground until the bombing campaign is over.

Elizabeth Well, thank you for your explanation, and for taking the time to walk me through it.

Eden Ma'am . . .

Eden gets to his feet. Bows from the neck. Is about to leave, when:

Elizabeth Before you go, I have one or two questions . . .

Eden smiles patronisingly.

When you mentioned the Israelis had launched the attack, you did not express surprise.

Eden Why would I express surprise?

Elizabeth Because from the transcripts of the Cabinet meetings of 23rd October it was clear that the Israeli position was that they would under no circumstances launch a full-scale attack by themselves for fear of diplomatic isolation. And yet they went on to do precisely that – launch an attack – indicating that either they changed their mind, or . . .

Eden Or . . . ?

Elizabeth Or . . . they weren't acting alone.

Eden looks up.

There was some kind of collusion.

The Queen stares unflinchingly at her Prime Minister.

Have we?

Eden Have we what?

Elizabeth Colluded with Israel? In any way?

Eden Ma'am?

Silence.

Elizabeth I ask because in the same Cabinet papers –

The Queen produces the appropriate papers.

– reference was made to a meeting you were proposing to attend the following day in Paris . . . which, by chance, the French and Israeli leaders would also be at. Obviously I was keen to follow up on this, but I then noticed in subsequent copies of the Cabinet minutes that any mention of that meeting in Paris had been redacted, leading me to believe that either it never took place, or –

Eden Or . . . ?

Elizabeth – people would prefer no one to know that it *had*.

Eden That first copy reached you?

Elizabeth It did.

Silence.

Don't forget, as Sovereign, I'm 'Copy Number One'.

Eden And 'Copy Number One' read it?

Elizabeth She did. She reads every piece of paper. That's in every box. Every day.

Eden's eyes close, then:

Eden Very well. Six days ago this government met with representatives of the French and Israeli governments in a small village on the outskirts of Paris, where a document was signed – the 'Sèvres Protocol' – which outlines plans for a coordinated offensive against Egypt whereby Israel would attack the Egyptian army near the Suez Canal . . .

Elizabeth With what justification?

Eden Every justification.

Elizabeth Are you sure this isn't just an irrational personal dislike?

Eden Certainly not.

Elizabeth An unjustifiable incursion into a sovereign nation to depose its leader and plunder its canal based on personal animosity?

Eden No.

Elizabeth Is it even *legal*?

Eden Let's keep the lawyers out of this.

Elizabeth Who knows about this?

Eden Individual members of the Cabinet. Senior members.

Elizabeth But not Parliament?

Eden No.

Elizabeth Or the United Nations?

Eden No.

Elizabeth When is this 'intervention' to take place?

Eden Tomorrow.

A stunned silence.

Elizabeth If this exercise is prosecuted successfully, what is the best possible outcome?

Eden That we rehabilitate a country ravaged by a maniacal tyrant, and reinstate a co-operative, friendly pro-Western government. An MI6 agent placed deep inside Egypt confidently predicts emancipated Egyptians will cheer our soldiers in the streets, and carry our generals on their shoulders.

Elizabeth And the worst possible outcome? That we lose the lives of British servicemen, and our reputation around the world for honesty and decency in matters of Foreign Policy.

The Queen notes Eden's increasingly agitated condition.

You seem – if you don't mind me saying – a little tired. Are you sleeping, Prime Minister?

Eden I'm fine. They've given me some stuff. To keep me going. Keep me sharp. On my feet.

Elizabeth Maybe they should give you some stuff to calm you down.

Eden They've given me some of that, too.

He looks at the Queen.

This is the right thing, you know. I was right about Hitler. I'm right about this fella.

Elizabeth You don't want to give it more time? And see if a diplomatic solution can be reached at the UN?

Eden No, Ma'am. The right thing is to go in now. And go in hard. (*A beat.*) Do I have your support?

The Queen stares at Eden.

Elizabeth The Prime Minister will always have my support.

Eden Thank you. Now, if Her Majesty will excuse me . . .

Eden bows, turns and goes.
    The Queen is left alone. She closes her eyes. Lost in thought. Her lips begins to mouth silent words.

Presently, the sound of a voice.

Young Elizabeth What are you doing?

It's the eleven-year-old Young Elizabeth, wearing a Girl Guide uniform, who has appeared on stage.

Elizabeth Praying. Or trying to.

Young Elizabeth Why don't you get on your knees?

Elizabeth Someone might walk in.

Young Elizabeth You get on your knees in your bedroom every morning, and every night.

Elizabeth That's my *bedroom*. It's private.

Young Elizabeth So is this room. It's even called the *Private* Audience Room.

Elizabeth No room with three doors and three windows should ever be called 'private'.

Young Elizabeth You're just proud! The Queen of England doesn't want to be seen on her knees.

Elizabeth Nonsense. Now shoo.

The Queen goes behind a mirror to change.

Why aren't you with the others, anyway?

Young Elizabeth It started raining, so we came inside. Do we *have* to have the troop meetings here at the Palace?

Elizabeth Yes.

Young Elizabeth And does there *have* to be a detective hovering *all* the time?

Elizabeth Yes.

Young Elizabeth And why can't the other girls just call me by my name?

Elizabeth No one will ever call you by your name. Nor look you in the eye when you're with them. Nor ask you what you think. Or believe. Or care about. They just expect you to do exactly as they want. Now, go on. Go back to the others. And don't show anyone you were sad.

Young Elizabeth I wasn't.

Elizabeth Yes, you were. But your secret's safe with me.

The Queen makes a three-fingered salute.

I promise.

Young Elizabeth goes. The Queen looks left and right, then gets on her knees . . .

Elizabeth Our father who art in heaven, hallowed be Thy name, Thy Kingdom come, Thy will be done, on earth as it is in heaven, give us this day our daily bread . . .

A figure in the doorway. It's the Queen's Private Secretary. He clears his throat.

Private Secretary Ma'am . . .? I just had a phone call from Downing Street to give us a bit of a heads-up.

Elizabeth About what?

Private Secretary It seems the Prime Minister left Number Ten somewhat troubled. Actually a little more than troubled. The word they used was 'vibrating' . . .

Elizabeth Oh.

Private Secretary Anyway they felt unable to predict with any degree of confidence the precise temperature of today's audience.

Elizabeth Are we for the high jump, do you suppose?

Private Secretary It's possible we are. Might be. (*Clears throat.*) Slightly.

At that moment, the Private Secretary's vast mobile telephone (the size of a book) rings. He excuses himself, then answers.

Hello? (*Listens.*) Yup. (*Listens.*) Right. (*Listens.*) Yup. (*Listens.*) Golly. (*Listens.*) Okay. Understood.

'Click': he hangs it up.

That was the guard from the King's Door, Ma'am, who says the Prime Minister has arrived.

Elizabeth What was the 'Golly'?

Private Secretary Ma'am?

Elizabeth You said 'Golly'!

Private Secretary Apparently the PM was out of the car before it had come to a halt, and stormed right past the Private Secretary in a fury.

Elizabeth (*raised eyebrow*) Golly.

A beat.

Well, then you'd better scram because if she's moving at that kind of speed by my reckoning she'll be here in . . .

Too late. A knock at the door. A breathless Equerry arrives, visibly terrified.
The door opens to reveal Margaret Thatcher, sixty-one, a woman at the height of her political career, a woman of almost equal iconic power to the Queen, and of near-identical age, born just six months before Elizabeth.
In the company of two such women, the two men, Equerry and Private Secretary, look at one another, then scarper for the exit in haste . . .
Mrs Thatcher and the Queen are left alone.
Mrs Thatcher curtsies slowly – exaggeratedly deeply, in a contrived, teeth-clenched gesture of reluctant deference.

Thatcher Your Majesty.

Elizabeth Prime Minister.

A silence. The Queen takes her seat. Mrs Thatcher remains standing. Vibrating.

Thatcher Before coming today I checked with the Cabinet Secretary and it turns out in the seven years since I have been Prime Minister we have had one hundred and thirty-three audiences – always the model of cordiality, productivity and mutual respect – so seen within a context like that it's perhaps not unreasonable to expect an isolated hiccup.

Elizabeth What 'hiccup?'

Thatcher I was under the impression that Her Majesty never expressed her political views in public . . .

Elizabeth I don't.

Thatcher That there was an unbreakable code of silence between Sovereign and First Minister.

Elizabeth There is. One, I should tell you, I have never broken. Not once in thirty-four years.

Thatcher Until now.

Elizabeth If you're referring to the *Sunday Times*, I had nothing to do with that story. I've always advised my Prime Ministers against reading newspapers . . .

Thatcher I *don't*, Ma'am –

Elizabeth They misunderstand, misquote, and misrepresent. Then everyone gets in a fluster.

Thatcher – but my Press Secretary does. And has working relationships with all the editors. And the editor in this case assured him the sources were 'unimpeachable'. (*A beat.*) 'Close to the Queen.' (*A beat.*) '*Very* close.' (*A beat.*) '*Unprecedentedly* close.'

The Queen averts her eyes.

And of course before running a story like this – a story with huge constitutional ramifications – the editor checked the story word by incriminating word, and it seems the '*unprecedentedly* close' sources 'inside the Palace' didn't backtrack *at all*! On the contrary, they offered one or two additions, encouraging the paper to go further!

Silence.

Elizabeth Well, I have no idea who is behind it all, but assure you a clarification will soon be forthcoming . . . along with the name of a culprit. In the meantime, should we not make a start on the business of the week? (*Checking watch.*) Only I'm mindful of the time . . .

Thatcher This *is* the business of the week, Ma'am. The *only* business – unless, that is, you'd prefer to focus on the latest revisions of the Airport Authority act of 1975, or the latest proposals by the Department of Education to bring the distribution of government grants to polytechnics more in line with the tax calendar . . .?

Silence.

I didn't think so.

The Queen averts her eyes.

It's not necessarily a bad thing, is it? Just for once? To break with tradition, and shed the straitjacket of our protocol to ask ourselves some of the bigger questions? I think we have enough respect for the institutions we both represent and for one another personally to do that. Once. Woman to woman. (*A beat.*) We are the same age, after all.

Elizabeth Are we?

Thatcher Just six months between us.

Elizabeth Who's the senior?

Thatcher (*an icy smile*) I am. Ma'am.

She opens her handbag, and produces a folded copy of the front page of the Sunday Times *from two days earlier.*

(*Reading.*) 'Uncaring, confrontational and socially divisive.' That's how these sources close to the Queen described me . . .

Elizabeth Prime Minister . . .

Thatcher That I . . . 'lack compassion and would be well advised to be more caring towards the less privileged in British society'.

She looks up.

I'm curious. If these 'sources' were pressed as to where this lack of compassion particularly caused offence, what would they say, do you imagine?

Elizabeth (*keen to change subject*) Couldn't we return to polytechnics, Prime Minister?

Thatcher The miners' strike, perhaps? The *Sunday Times* suggested 'some in the Palace' held that the policies of my government had done 'irretrievable damage to the country's social fabric' . . .

Silence.

Let me remind Her Majesty, that she may remind the 'sources' so close to her, when we came to power, the dead lay unburied and the sick languished in corridors on hospital trolleys unattended because unelected union leaders had called their workers out on strike in an attempt to bring down a government . . . substituting the rule of the *mob* for the rule of the law. I made the pledge then that *no* union leaders would *ever* succeed in holding this great country to ransom again. And they *have* not succeeded.

Elizabeth Prime Minister . . .

Thatcher It takes a very special kind of courage to cross a hostile picket line every day to feed your family – men like that are what we are proud to call 'the best of British' . . .

The Queen looks away.

But above all else it seems the Palace took offence to my stance regarding sanctions against South Africa.

'South Africa': the words ring out like a gunshot in the room. The Queen sits up.

Ma'am, let us be quite clear about this. *Nothing* useful can be achieved by sanctions.

The Queen's tone has noticeably changed. Tougher. More resolute. Colder.

Elizabeth Sanctions would hit the apartheid regime where it hurts.

Thatcher They would hit *us*, too. South Africa is the UK's fourth largest trading partner.

Elizabeth I was hoping we might look at it from their point of view.

Thatcher I am . . . *Ma'am*. South Africa is already a disinvestment economy. A total ban would devastate them.

Elizabeth Black South Africans *want* sanctions. Shouldn't we listen to them?

Thatcher Black South Africans don't want to inherit a wasteland.

Elizabeth 'They will if they feel it's *their* wasteland.' President Kaunda of Zambia. You could do worse than talk to him. He would confirm as much.

Thatcher It is not the business of a British Prime Minister to consult with tinpot dictators!

The Queen looks up, flashes with indignation.

Elizabeth But it *is* of their Sovereign when they are part of the Commonwealth.

Thatcher Ah, the Commonwealth!

Elizabeth Yes. The Commonwealth.

Thatcher I recognise that for your family the transition of this nation from Empire to comparative supplicancy on the world stage may have come as a greater shock than to the rest of us. But I would argue that the Commonwealth is not the way to fill that gap, or restore that loss of self-esteem. There *are* ways of Britain being great again – and that is through a revitalised economy, renewed economic power, not through political fraternisation with unreliable tribal leaders in eccentric costumes . . .

Elizabeth But isn't that all I am, Prime Minister? A tribal leader? In eccentric costume?

Thatcher Certainly not! You're Head of an evolved Constitutional Monarchy that stretches back to William the Conqueror. It's not comparing like with like.

Elizabeth But that's where we differ. You see, Prime Minister, I consider myself *exactly* like them. To me Ghana, Zambia, Malawi are great sovereign nations. With great histories. I'm aware you probably don't share that view. That to you the Commonwealth is something of a distraction. A waste of time. I gather there's even an acronym you use for the annual Commonwealth Heads of Government Meeting which is so important to me.

Thatcher averts her eyes.

What was it again?

Thatcher 'Compulsory Handouts for Greedy Mendicants'?

Elizabeth Actually that's somewhat politer than the one I heard. (*A beat.*) 'Coons Holidaying on Government Money'?

Thatcher I had nothing to do with that! That was my husband!

Elizabeth The Commonwealth of Nations is an idea that is dear to my heart. In a way I have given my life to it. That was the pledge I made forty years ago.

Thatcher I remember listening to it. On the wireless. We were both so young at the time. Just girls.

Elizabeth As Sovereign I am obliged to support you as Prime Minister. On *any* position you take. Including South Africa. Including sanctions. Your position is that of the Government, that of the United Kingdom, and that's the end of it. I will fall in line. My question is, given the lack of impact it has on your day-to-day political fortunes, and yet how important it is to me, couldn't you have supported *me* just once? My fellow Heads of Government in the Commonwealth, many of whom I consider friends, feel I have betrayed them on the most important issue to them.

Thatcher All they need do is read the *Sunday Times*. (*Indicating newspaper.*) It will leave them in no doubt as to your position.

   Silence.

My responsibility for the time I have in office is to put sentimentality to one side and look after this country's interests from the perspective of a cold balance sheet – pros and cons – and it is my judgement that to focus on *our* economy and *our* standing in the world would be best for Britain *and* incidentally the profile of the person that personifies it.

Elizabeth You, Prime Minister.

Thatcher No, *you*, Ma'am. You'll be here having these conversations long after I've gone.

Thatcher stares at the Queen.

And while I greatly admire your sense of fairness and compassion for those less fortunate than us –

Elizabeth Do you, really?

Thatcher – let's not forget of the two of us I am the one that came from a small street. In an irrelevant town. With nothing. We had no hot water. We had to heat it in a copper. My mother made all our clothes. And I don't want people's pity, or charity or compassion. Nothing would insult me more.

Elizabeth Not everybody is as strong as you, Prime Minister. Or prodigiously gifted. Or driven. I can't help thinking about the rest of us sometimes. Those that are just . . . normal. That have to read things twice to understand. That need a prevailing wind to get through life. And rarely get it.

The Queen smiles.

I expect in your eyes that makes me a 'wet'. That *is* the word, isn't it? That you scribble in the margins of your Cabinet papers? When someone says something you don't agree with?

Thatcher I came to office with one deliberate intent, to change this country from being a dependent to a self-reliant culture, and I think in that I have succeeded. Britons now instinctively understand there is no longer such a thing as society. They have learned to look after number one, use their elbows, get ahead. And are richer for it. No one would remember the Good Samaritan if he'd only had good intentions. You see, he had money as well.

She checks her watch.

Our time is up. How it flies.

Silence.

You must be very much looking forward to tomorrow. The wedding? Prince Andrew and Sarah Ferguson.

Elizabeth Yes, we are.

Thatcher They seem like a good match.

Elizabeth Yes. We think so.

They get to their feet.

Thatcher My own son, Mark, announced recently that he would be getting married.

Elizabeth The explorer?

Thatcher Not an explorer, Ma'am. That was just once. He's a businessman. An entrepreneur.

Elizabeth Oh, yes. And who is the lucky lady?

Thatcher An American. From Texas.

Elizabeth Arms, wasn't it? Your entrepreneur son?

Thatcher Not any more. He's moved into cars now. And fixing.

Elizabeth Oh, a mechanic? Like me. I trained in the war.

Thatcher Not that kind of 'fixing', Ma'am. It means he makes introductions.

Elizabeth (*not understanding*) To whom?

Thatcher Businesses. From the Middle East, mostly. And South Africa.

Elizabeth Of course.

Thatcher goes, leaving the Queen alone on stage.
Behind her, Young Elizabeth appears, and addresses the nation . . .

Young Elizabeth As I speak to you today from Cape Town I am six thousand miles from the country where I was born. But I am certainly not six thousand miles from home. That is the great privilege of belonging to a worldwide Commonwealth. We must not be daunted by the anxieties and hardships that the war has left behind for us all.

The Queen exits the stage, and Young Elizabeth walks forward, continuing her broadcast.

Young Elizabeth If we all go forward with an unwavering faith, a high courage and a quiet heart, we shall be able to make of this ancient Commonwealth, which we all love so dearly, an even grander thing – more free, more prosperous, more happy and a more powerful influence for good in the world – than it has been in the greatest days of our forefathers. To accomplish that we must give nothing less than the whole of ourselves. There is a motto which has been borne by many of my ancestors – a noble motto: 'I serve.' I should like to make that dedication now. It is very simple.

The Queen reappears on stage. She is now an eighty-six-year-old woman. Her eyesight is no longer what it was, nor her mobility. She moves more slowly, her knee giving her trouble. Her back is an almost constant source of pain.

Young Elizabeth I declare before you all that my whole life, whether it be long or short, shall be devoted to your service and the service of our great imperial family to which we all belong.

Young Elizabeth exits.

It's 2013. The door opens and the Equerry comes in. The sound of a ringing mobile telephone, with a 'Gangnam Style' ringtone.

Equerry The Prime Minister, Ma'am.

David Cameron, forty-six, enters, bows respectfully.

Cameron Your Majesty.

The 'Gangnam Style' ringing continues.

Elizabeth Are you going to answer that?

Cameron Not me.

The Queen looks at the Equerry.

Equerry (*hands raised in innocence*) Nor me, Ma'am.

Elizabeth (*realising*) Oh, for heaven's sake . . .

The Queen moves with difficulty. Searches in her pockets. Finds the phone. Tries to turn it off.

Grandchildren.

Cameron May I, Ma'am?

Cameron takes it and switches it off for her.

Elizabeth How did you do that?

Cameron The red button, here, Ma'am.

He presses the keyboard. The Queen squints.

Elizabeth There isn't a red button.

Cameron It disappears after you touch it.

The Queen stares. Bemused. Confounded.

Cameron (*indicates*) Nice.

Elizabeth What?

Cameron The new Samsung.

Elizabeth I begged them not to give me one, but then security persuaded me it doubled as a useful tracking device in case I try to escape. I expect you have one, too?

Cameron Four.

Elizabeth Four? How awful. Anyway, we have more important things to discuss than this. Welcome back, Prime Minster.

Cameron Thank you, Ma'am.

Elizabeth We followed your progress in the papers. All seemed to go well . . . in Bonn. Or was it Bern?

Cameron Basle. I think so.

Elizabeth I seem to do nothing *but* welcome you back from European summits. How many have you been to now?

Cameron Lost count.

Elizabeth Me, too. So . . . where do you think we are *now*? In a nutshell?

Cameron The will for the euro to survive is there, no question. And the core countries, France, Germany, are finally taking the steps they need to in terms of banking union and federalism. But I still don't get a sense of a shared mission.

Unseen by Cameron the Queen has nodded off . . . .

Or ideology. Or anyone doing it because they actually *believe* in it in the way the previous generation of politicians did. It just feels like they're all doing it solely to avoid calamity . . . Eurogeddon. It's hard to understand why we British have been so resistant to Europe . . . historically.

Cameron notices the Queen is asleep...

Mostly . . . I'd say it's because we're an island, and not physically part of the continent. And that we have too vivid a memory of the war –

The Queen sits up at mention of this.

– and struggle with the languages. Not to mention the fact that we . . .

The Queen shakes herself awake.

Elizabeth – tend not to like them very much.

Cameron Quite. But don't you think it might also be the fact that in *you* –

Elizabeth Oh. My fault again . . .

Cameron – we have a Head of State who has such strong emotional ties with the Commonwealth that it's impossible for us ever, as subjects, to commit ourselves fully to any *other* union. That is, until you –

Elizabeth Drop dead?

Cameron No. No. No. (*Hesitates.*) Actually, *yes* . . . and it's possible for our relationship with the Commonwealth to be redrawn.

Elizabeth It's true. I instinctively feel closer to Africans than Europeans. I was even called 'The African Queen'. Kenneth Kaunda of Zambia, or Julius Nyerere of Tanzania, these were men one looked forward to seeing. One could do business with them. Do you feel the same way about Mrs Merkel? Or Monsieur Hollande? Do you *like* them?

Cameron I don't *hate* them.

Elizabeth I suppose that's an answer of sorts.

Cameron She asked about the baby, yesterday. Chancellor Merkel. They all do.

Elizabeth What baby? Oh, *the* baby? Yes, twenty weeks. We had a scan. You can see everything now. In 3D. Nails growing. Eyelashes. Very exciting. In my day, they'd just listen to one's heartbeat, take one's blood pressure and tell one to get on with it.

Cameron Will Her Majesty share the secret with me?

Elizabeth Of what?

Cameron The gender.

Elizabeth Certainly not. You'd only take it to the bookmakers to cash in!

Cameron I hear the odds favour a little Princess.

Elizabeth Absolute nonsense. Based on what? Makes no difference, anyway. Boy or girl, it's still headed for the top job. One day. (*A beat.*) If this all still exists then.

The Queen tails off, then notices something.

Goodness . . . Are you wearing make-up?

Cameron No.

She slowly walks over to scrutinise Cameron.

Elizabeth Yes, you are! It's come off your neck, on to your collar.

Cameron Oh, that was from an interview this morning.

Elizabeth They didn't offer to take it off?

Cameron They did, but there was no time.

Elizabeth That's the excuse Mr Blair used to give. By the end, I noticed, he wore it all the time. (*Shudders.*) Along with that grin.

A beat.

You're a great admirer, aren't you?

Cameron Of Tony's? Say what you like about him, he was jolly good at the game. Ran rings round us for years.

Elizabeth My husband couldn't stand him. Is that *very* indiscreet?

Cameron Yes.

Elizabeth (*covers her mouth ironically*) Ooops.

Cameron How is His Highness?

Elizabeth Better, thank you. Up on his feet and stalking. But no shooting himself – doctor's orders. The recoil from the gun could dislodge the stent that's keeping him alive.

Cameron Oh.

Elizabeth Yes. We're both showing wear and tear now. But still hanging on.

   A beat.

Just.

   A beat.

A bit like your arrangement with the Liberal Democrats.

   Cameron's smile fades.

I think it was Disraeli who said the British don't care for coalitions.

Cameron Nor you, Ma'am.

Elizabeth (*struggling to hear*) What's that?

Cameron (*louder*) Nor you, Ma'am?

Elizabeth Did I say as much?

Cameron Not in as many words.

Elizabeth (*irritated*) Well, then.

Cameron But one thing I think you'll find all your Prime Ministers agree on – is you have a way of saying nothing yet making your view perfectly clear.

Elizabeth I think I'd care for it more if I felt the people had *voted* for it. Had you formed your coalition first and gone to the country that would have been a different matter.

The Queen starts cleaning her glasses.

Cameron You know, thinking about all your previous PMs just now, how many have there been?

Elizabeth Twelve. The Dirty Dozen. I'm a record breaker. More even than Queen Victoria. Churchill, Eden, Macmillan, Douglas-Home, Wilson, Heath, Thatcher, Major, Blair, Brown . . . (*Indicates.*) Cameron.

The Queen hesitates.

I've forgotten one . . .

Cameron No, I was counting. You got them all.

Voice No, she didn't.

A bespectacled, avuncular white-haired man in his late sixties walks on.

Callaghan James Callaghan. Labour Prime Minister, 1976 to 79.

Crestfallen, Callaghan turns to the Queen.

How could you, Ma'am? You remembered Alec Douglas-Home? How long was he in Downing Street? A *year*?

Elizabeth That's different. He was a friend.

Callaghan You remembered Ted Heath.

Elizabeth Someone has to.

Callaghan Was I really that forgettable?

Elizabeth No, not at all . . .

Callaghan In the time I was in office, we met almost seventy times.

Elizabeth Yes.

Callaghan You always said how much you enjoyed our sessions.

Elizabeth I did. Very much.

Callaghan I gave you a coffee pot!

Elizabeth The coffee pot!

Callaghan Audrey picked it out. 'Sunny Jim', you called me!

Elizabeth Yes.

Callaghan 'If we have to prove our Europeanism by accepting French as the dominant language then my position is clear. *Non merci beaucoup*.' (*A beat.*) You always said how much you enjoyed that.

Elizabeth I did. Very much.

Callaghan rolls his eyes, and exits. Cameron continues, unaware.

Cameron An unbroken line. From Churchill to me. Extraordinary.

Elizabeth And beyond. I'm not done yet. To be Queen of England is not a job or a shift you put in. It's a duty consecrated by the grace of God. My working life *is* my natural life. They are indivisible . . . so I'm afraid you're saddled with me until He takes me. Or the revolution. Whichever comes first.

Cameron We aren't much good at revolutions in this country.

Elizabeth Don't think that fact's gone unappreciated in this house.

Cameron Of the twelve, was there one . . . with whom the working relationship was . . . particularly fruitful?

Elizabeth You mean did I have a favourite?

Cameron I suppose that *is* what I'm asking.

Elizabeth What a question! 'Friendliness, not friendship', Mr Cameron. That's the principle. 'The office not the individual'. Now, if there's nothing else . . . we'll see one another next week?

Cameron takes his cue. Gets to his feet.

Cameron We will. Budget week.

Elizabeth Should I be frightened? I've heard renewed rumours of that mansion tax.

The Queen gets to her feet with difficulty. Appears frail.

Cameron Nothing to worry about. Unless you've put them all in the name of a company in one of your overseas territories.

Elizabeth I'm afraid we don't have many of those left.

Cameron smiles, bows, and goes. The Queen's smile fades. But rather than follow him, she remains seated. Her Equerry appears in the doorway.

Equerry Staying, Ma'am?

Elizabeth Yes. Not going anywhere. It's what I do best, apparently. 'The unbroken line,' that's what he called me. 'The constant presence.' 'What was her achievement?' the historians will ask. She lived long, showed up, cut ribbons, and knew when to keep her head down and her mouth shut. A postage stamp with a pulse. (*A beat.*) Have I, by the way?

Equerry Have you what, Ma'am?

Elizabeth Had a favourite Prime Minister?

The Equerry looks aghast.

Elizabeth Don't look like that. I know what gossips you lot are . . .

The Dressers walk on.

I must have let something slip . . .

Equerry If you *were* to believe the gossip . . . there was *one* you cared for more than all the rest.

Elizabeth Who?

The door opens. Two tall, thick-set men burst in with Harold Wilson.

Wilson Quickly, before she comes.

Security Man Prime Minister, the Palace has their own security . . .

Wilson That's the point. Their security has been *breached*, don't you understand? I want the whole room checked. Picture frames, telephones, mirrors . . .

Security Man Sir, we don't have the authority to do this.

Wilson The *chairs*, Sergeant. And then the chandelier. Or must I do it myself?

It's September 1975. Wilson is Prime Minister once again, and back in Downing Street having narrowly defeated Edward Heath in two 1974 elections.
The strain of leading his own party and a minority government through a troubled decade shows on Wilson's face. He is pale. His hair is whiter. He has visibly aged.

Wilson Don't be alarmed, Ma'am. These gentlemen are with me. I've asked them to check the room.

The Detectives start examining the phone and lights.

Elizabeth Whatever for?

Wilson covers his lips, indicating 'Shh'.
   He goes to the Queen's notepad, pulls out a pen,
and writes something on it.
   Wilson passes the Queen the pad. She reads it.

(*Horrified.*) No!

Wilson nods solemnly.

By whom?

Wilson writes another note on the pad of paper.

That's absurd.

Wilson Sadly not, Ma'am.

Wilson writes another note. Longer. He hands it to the
Queen. The Queen reads it, then:

Elizabeth But we have our own security here. How
would they have got in?

Wilson On this occasion I believe they posed as . . .

Wilson writes another note.

Elizabeth (*blurts out*) Decorators?

Wilson Yes, Ma'am. When the Audience Room was
redecorated recently.

Elizabeth I hate to disappoint you – but this room has
not been redecorated in years.

Wilson Are you sure?

Wilson goes to examine the paint on the wall.

Elizabeth That paint has not been touched since my
grandfather, George V.

The Detectives look up.

Detective That's it, sir. All clear. Clean as a whistle.

Wilson Really? You've checked the table light? And the phone?

Detective Yes, sir.

Wilson Behind the paintings?

Detective All done, sir.

Wilson The Gainsborough?

Detective (*an awkward silence*) Nothing.

The two Detectives bow in respect to the Queen, and retreat out of the room.

Wilson sits down. Shaken. For the first time it's apparent not all is well. He is not the same man. He whispers gravely to himself, barely audible:

Wilson God . . . what's happening to me?

A silence.

If I had any doubts before I came today, those doubts have now gone. (*A beat.*) I can't go on, Ma'am. Not like this.

Elizabeth What are you talking about?

Wilson This is no way for a leader to be. Forgetting some things. Imagining others.

Elizabeth It's age. Happens to us all.

Wilson No. It's not just age, Ma'am.

A poignant silence.

It's been diagnosed. And has a name.

Silence.

I first noticed it a few months ago. At the Lord Mayor's dinner. I always speak without notes. Suddenly I dried. Had difficulty expressing myself. Then Mary told me I was misplacing things. Had become more subdued. So I went to see a doctor. Didn't tell anyone. Pretended it was for my back.

Elizabeth What did the doctor say?

Wilson That the symptoms I described could be exhaustion, could be age, but more likely were classic indicators of . . . Alzheimer's. They told me to keep an eye out for increasing memory loss. Lack of judgement. Personality changes . . . (*Tailing off.*) Imagining rooms had been painted and bugged – for example.

Silence.

Elizabeth I wouldn't worry. Several of your predecessors had *far* more serious afflictions and continued to govern without the public being any the wiser.

Wilson Is that supposed to comfort me? No, Ma'am, it's a mental health issue now, and belongs in the hands of professionals.

Elizabeth But you forgetting things makes you just like the rest of us. Balmoral, a few years ago. The book belonging to my husband's sister. The way you memorised that . . .

Wilson (*remembering*) *Life in a Top Regiment* . . .

Elizabeth *Crack* Regiment . . .

Wilson 'A Novel of German Military . . .'

Elizabeth (*prompting*) '. . . Manners and Morals.'

The Queen stares.

Have you shared this concern with anyone else?

Wilson No one. Not even Mary.

Elizabeth I suppose I should ask . . . what the next step would be?

Wilson I will inform the Cabinet Secretary of my decision to resign. That will trigger a leadership election within the party.

Elizabeth It will come as a *terrible* shock.

Wilson Maybe. But no shock lasts longer than forty-eight hours. There is too much appetite for the next shock.

Silence.

I never wanted to go on beyond sixty anyway. That's long enough in any job, especially one in public life.

Elizabeth Is that a hint?

Wilson Certainly not. There's a surfeit of good people available to take over my job. Not so many for yours.

Elizabeth Now, now . . .

Wilson C'mon, don't pretend you don't agree. The way he shoots his mouth off and gallivants around it's hard to imagine you and the Prince of Wales are from the same family – let alone mother and son.

Elizabeth I'm sorry. Was that a compliment?

Wilson It was. But it was from Huddersfield. So it came in through the tradesman's entrance.

The Queen smiles. A silence.

Elizabeth I will miss our sessions. I don't mind admitting I let out an unconstitutional cheer when you beat Mr Heath this time.

Wilson I always said you were a leftie at heart.

Elizabeth Nothing to do with the politics. You're just a better companion, that's all. Though I didn't imagine I'd ever say *that* when we first met.

Wilson No. You thought I was going to rough you lot up. And look what a softie I turned out to be.

Wilson smiles. They get up. The Queen manages a smile.

Elizabeth So we'll continue as normal. (*She hesitates.*) At least for the time being?

Wilson Yes.

Elizabeth See you next week.

The Queen extends her hand.

Wilson Not next week, Ma'am. It's the by-election, if you remember.

Elizabeth Oh, yes. Woolwich West. They're expecting that to be close.

Wilson A perfectly safe Labour seat. Our man had held it for eleven years. Then he drops dead. Hill-walking. (*A beat.*) I could have murdered him.

The Queen laughs. Wilson's smile fades.

Elizabeth What's the matter?

Wilson I've forgotten his name.

Now it's undeniable. No more brave smiles.

Elizabeth Oh Prime Minister. William Hamling.

A silence.

Wilson Of course. (*Fighting tears.*) Thank you, Ma'am.

Wilson bows low, with difficulty, but genuine deference, then goes. Before he reaches the door:

85

Elizabeth (*calling after him*) Prime Minister . . . ?

Wilson turns in the doorway.

If you saw fit to invite your Queen to supper at Downing Street before you left, she would be delighted.

Wilson stops, and stares, realising the significance.

Wilson But that's an honour previously only given to Churchill.

Elizabeth The Duke of Edinburgh and I would like that very much.

Wilson So would Mrs Wilson and I.

He turns and goes.

The Queen is left alone. Sad to see him go. A fifty-year-old woman. She goes to the window. Looks out. As always, taking care to hide to one side so she cannot be seen.
Presently the little eleven-year-old Elizabeth comes in with two dogs. Corgis.

Young Elizabeth You still here?

Elizabeth Yes.

Young Elizabeth Anything interesting?

Elizabeth Not really. A dog chasing pigeons.

They both crane their necks.

What have you been up to today?

Young Elizabeth Just had a lesson.

Elizabeth With Vice-Provost Marten?

Young Elizabeth Yes.

Elizabeth What was the lesson about?

Young Elizabeth (*rolls eyes, bored*) 'The British Prime Minister'.

Elizabeth And what did you learn?

Young Elizabeth pulls out a notebook.

Young Elizabeth Mainly what a strange creature he is. Marked by shyness. (*Reading.*) 'Often lonely and unhappy at school, having suffered a trauma in childhood – leaving them haunted by a compulsive and obsessive need for love and power.' (*A beat.*) Basically they're all mad.

Elizabeth What advice did he offer on how to deal with them?

Young Elizabeth To keep my opinions to myself. Remember my constitutional limitations at all times. And hope that I may nudge them by maybe one or two degrees . . . over time. (*Rolls eyes.*) How humiliating.

Elizabeth Why?

Young Elizabeth To have to sit there like a stuffed animal and listen politely to mad people for hours on end –

Elizabeth That's one version of it. A kinder one, perhaps, would be that you're allowing complicated people, *over*-complicated people to measure themselves against something unchanging. Permanent. Simple. Your ordinariness as a human being will be your greatest asset as a sovereign. A more distinctive, perhaps imaginative person would make a mess of it. And if I would add anything to your lesson it's this: those 'mad people' will prove to be your greatest allies. No matter how old-fashioned, expensive and unjustifiable we are, we will *still* be preferable to a elected president meddling in what they do. Which is why they always dive in to rescue us every time we make a mess of things. If you want to know how it is that the monarchy in this country has survived as long as it has – don't look to its monarchs. Look to its Prime Ministers.

A beat.

Now c'mon. You need to get back to Kingfisher Patrol.

The Queen and Young Elizabeth exit.
A moment later, the Queen pops her head back into the room, tutting at her own wastefulness, and . . .
'Click': turns out the light.